READ & PLAY™
INDIAN
TABLA
DRUMS

for Students, Teachers and Percussionists
by Kuljit Bhamra

MODULE 2 Combined Sounds and Advanced Techniques

keda MUSIC

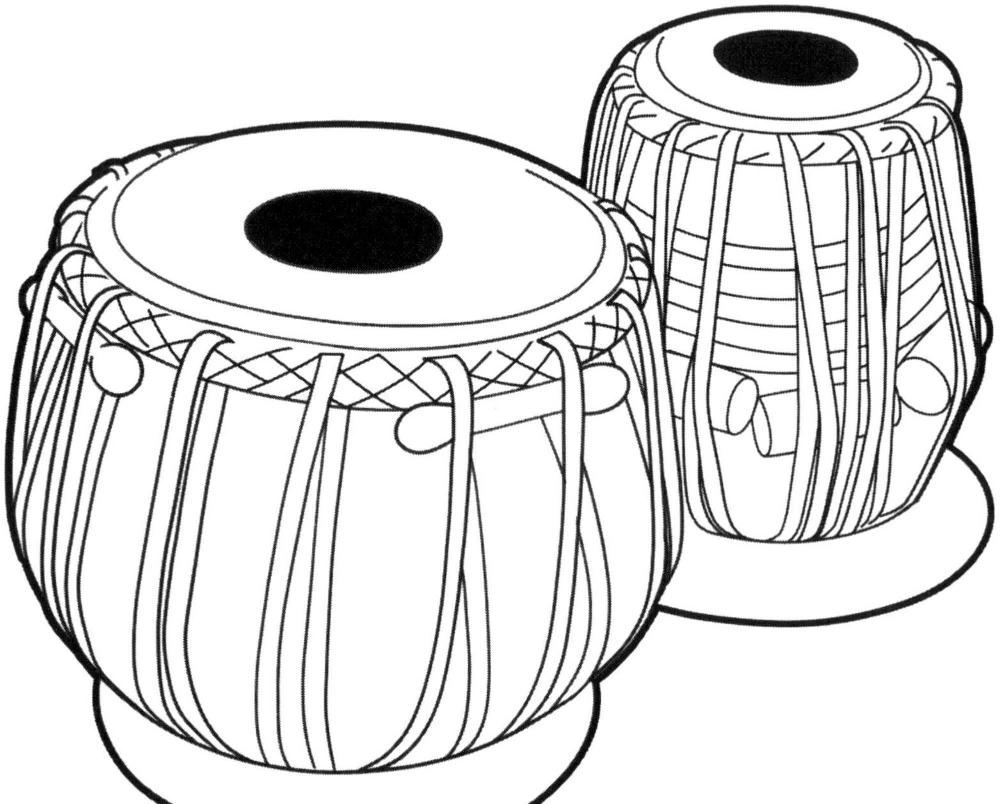

FOREWORD

The exciting and revolutionary Universal Indian Drum Notation used in this course allows students, teachers, composers and musicians to play the tabla and enjoy its rich, beautiful sounds.

This breakthrough in tabla-education makes the instrument more accessible to musicians from differing backgrounds and cultures.

In this course, easy to follow modules include Practice exercises and Solo pieces. In addition, specially written Group pieces have been designed for tabla with other classroom instruments.

A music teacher armed with these books will be able to bring the sounds of Indian tabla drums to the school and stage.

I hope that you have fun learning and playing the tabla!

Kuljit Bhamra

COURSE OVERVIEW

MODULE 1

Discovering the Basic Sounds

Large Drum – Closed and Open Sounds
Smaller Drum – Closed and Open Sounds
Practice Pieces
Solo Pieces
Group Pieces

MODULE 2

Combined Sounds and Advanced Techniques

Large Drum – the sound *Gi* and Slides
Smaller Drum – sounds *Ta* and *Ti*
Both Drums – combined sounds *Da* and *Di*
Practice Pieces
Solo Pieces
Group Pieces

MODULE 3

Rolls, Tremolos and Traditional Rhythms

Rolls and Tremolos
Traditional Rhythms
Practice Pieces
Solo Pieces
Group Pieces

First published 2017
Copyright © by Keda Music Ltd
ISBN 978-0-244-30942-8

All rights reserved. No part of this publication may be reproduced, stored in a retrieval system, or transmitted in any form or any means, electronic, mechanical, photocopying, recording or otherwise, without the permission of Keda Music Ltd

CONTENTS

Course Overview

Acknowledgements

The Author

MODULE 2 INTRODUCTION 8

LARGE DRUM 10
Muted Open Sound – *Gi* 10
Slide (*Glissando*) 14

SMALLER DRUM 22
Muted Open Sound – *Ta* 22
Muted Closed Sound – *Ti* 26

BOTH DRUMS – COMBINED SOUNDS 28
Da 28
Di 32

SOLO PIECES 37
Tabla Solo 4 38
Tabla Solo 5 39
Tabla Solo 6 40

GROUP PIECES 43
Group Piece 5 44
Group Piece 6 50
Group Piece 7 54

STRIKES & SOUNDS 63

ACKNOWLEDGEMENTS

Kuljit Bhamra would like to thank the following for their support in refining and road-testing his Read & Play™ system throughout its ten years of development.

ORGANISATIONS

Sound and Music, SPNM: Ed McKeon, Barbara Palczynski, Nicole Rochman, Judith Robinson, Susanna Eastburn, Richard Whitelaw.

Jas Musicals: Harjit Singh Shah

Central Research Laboratory, Hayes

TABLA PLAYERS

Subhankar Banerjee, Gurdain Singh Rayatt, Sandeep Raval, Dharmesh Parmar.

PERCUSSIONISTS, MUSICIANS

Magnus Mehta, Joley Cragg, Adam Clifford, Scott Lumsdaine, Manny Arciniega, Dan Bradley, Joe Richards, Paul Clarvis, Becky Brass, Matt Arnold, Felicity Scott.

EDUCATIONAL INSTITUTIONS

Purcell School of Music: Alison Cox OBE, Kevin Hathway
Trinity Laban Conservatoire: Gary Kettel
Royal Academy of Music: Neil Percy
Royal College of Music: David Hockings
Alchemy Festival: Dr Sophie Ransby
Birmingham Conservatoire: Adrian Spillett
Darbar Arts: Sandeep Virdee

COMPOSERS, ORCHESTRATORS AND CONDUCTORS

Howard Goodall CBE, Chris Nightingale, Robert Ziegler, Simon Nathan, Jataneel Banerjee, Evangelia Rigaki, Roberto Rusconi.

Special thanks to Professor Jerri Daboo of the University of Exeter without whose passion and consistent support this book would not exist.

Satpaul Bhamra and Anna MacKenzie, book design
Ammy Phull, photography

THE AUTHOR

One of the most inspiring musicians in the British Indian music scene, Kuljit Bhamra is a self taught composer, tabla player and record producer with an extensive musical repertoire.

His name has become synonymous with vibrant percussion performances and he is widely acknowledged as being the pioneering name behind the Bhangra phenomenon. He is the recipient of many awards including a platinum disc for outstanding record sales by the former much-loved radio DJ, John Peel. In 2009 he was honoured with an MBE for services to Bhangra and Brit-Asian music.

Kuljit is known for his passion for combining instruments and music from different genres and cultural backgrounds. His unique ability to translate western scores and compositions for Indian musicians enables him to work in a wide range of the industry including theatre, film soundtracks, jazz, western classical and education. He has performed worldwide with artists including Rais Khan, Jagjit Singh, Sultan Khan, Ghulam Ali, Luke Haynes, Andy Sheppard, Mike Lindup, Britten Sinfonia, BBC Concert Orchestra, Bobby McFarren, The Sugababes and Shakira.

With over 40 years of experience, he has worked both independently and collaboratively on film scores including the soundtrack for the award-winning *Bhaji on the Beach*, *A Winter of Love*, *Bend It Like Beckham* and appeared on *The Guru*, *The Four Feathers*, *Brick Lane*, *Charlie And The Chocolate Factory*, *A Little Princess*, *Wings of a Dove*, *Jadoo* and Channel 4's *Indian Summers*. In 2002 Kuljit worked on Andrew Lloyd Webber's hit musical *Bombay Dreams* as on-stage percussionist, and then went on to write the Indian music for the West End musical *The Far Pavilions*. It was at this time that he began to develop his revolutionary tabla notation system so that his deputies could accurately play what he had written for the show. The notation system was used fully in the musical adaptation of *Bend It Like Beckham* in which Kuljit performed as part of the onstage band.

Kuljit's Universal Indian Drum Notation used in these books makes it possible for composers to write for tabla, dholak and dhol players, and share it with others worldwide. It also enables music students to have an intuitive hands-on approach by following written exercises. This is a breakthrough in tabla education and makes the instrument more accessible. It also allows music teachers to be able to teach the tabla by following a standardised, methodical approach.

In his mission to demystify Indian music, Kuljit created Keda Music Ltd in 2016 with industrial designer Graham England and product developer Phil Eddershaw. Brought together by their passion for music, they are committed to creating new ways for musicians to access the beautiful sounds of Indian drums through a range of unique electronic instruments, educational tools and workshops.

MODULE 2 INTRODUCTION

This is the second in the series of our Read & Play™ books intended to introduce you to the world of the Indian tabla drum. The learning process has been designed to suit the self-sufficient learner who has a basic knowledge of western music notation.

IMPORTANT
Grasp the techniques in this Module before progressing to Module 3.

In this module, we will learn how to play *combination sounds* created by striking both drums simultaneously. We will also study some *advanced techniques* that will enable you to create new open and closed sounds on each drum. These include the iconic glissando slide played on the large tabla drum.

It is assumed that you have already studied the techniques and exercises in Module 1. Once you have worked through the exercises and pieces in this module, you will be fully prepared to study new techniques and traditional rhythms in Module 3.

COURSE METHOD AND TOOLS

Universal Indian Drum Notation

The notation system used in this course operates in a similar way to a regular two-line bongo stave. For Indian drums, each sound has its own unique notehead and position on the stave. These are described in detail throughout Modules 1 and 2 and also summarised in the Strikes & Sounds chart at the back of this book.

The system applies to all Indian two-headed drums including *Dholak*, *Mridangam*, *Dhol*, *Tavil* and *Pakhavaj*.

We at Keda Music hope that our exciting products, together with this new method of teaching, will bring the tabla into a more widely accessible and modern context.

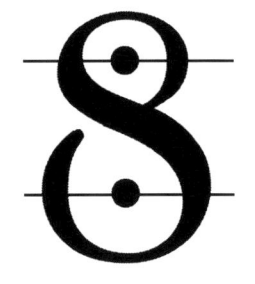

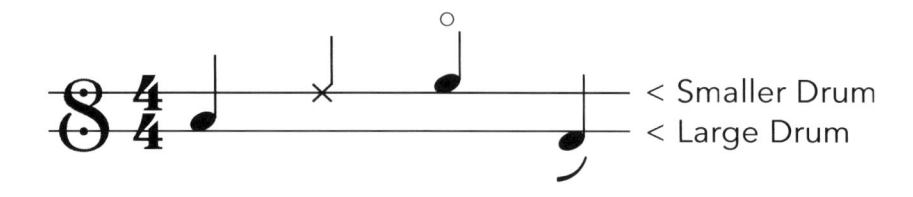

Indian Drum Clef

Simple Learning Process

The playing techniques in this course are explained in *easy to understand steps*.

Each module is divided into three sections:

- *Practice pieces* to learn the basic strikes and sounds.
- *Solo pieces* to develop your skill in performing.
- *Group pieces* specially composed to perform alongside classroom instruments such as recorder, djembe, shaker and glockenspiel.

Practice Time allows you to develop your techniques slowly and steadily with a metronome and suggested tempos. When you feel ready, have fun and *Play Along* with the online backing tracks.

Online at keda.co.uk > Learn & Support

- *Play Along* backing tracks for all Practice, Solo and Group pieces. There are two versions of each piece – with and without the recorded tabla.
- *Scores & Parts* to download (for free) and print as required
- *Strikes & Sounds* of techniques and notations with videos.

Practice Time
Choose a speed that works for you

Play Along
Have fun with online backing tracks

Strikes & Sounds
Review techniques and watch them online

Scores & Parts
Download and print your music

ONLINE

Video resources are provided to support you at every level.
keda.co.uk

COURSE FEEDBACK

Please feel free to contact us with any questions or comments that you may have.
info@keda.co.uk

LARGE DRUM

Large Drum **Muted Open Sound** Gi

The sound *Gi* (pronounced as in *gig*) is an open sound that is heavily dampened. The strike is very like *Ge*, but with extra pressure applied by the heel of the hand. The resulting sound is a short, muted open sound which is higher in pitch than *Ge*.

Follow these steps to play *Gi*:

• Start with the *resting position*.

• Raise your fingers by flexing your wrist and arc your hand as if holding an invisible tennis ball above the black spot.

• Press down onto the drumhead with the heel of your hand.

• Bring your arched hand downwards so that the tip of your middle finger strikes the drum on the skin above the black spot. Allow your finger to *bounce off* naturally.

• Immediately roll your heel off the drumhead by rotating your wrist away from you. This enables the drum to resonate.

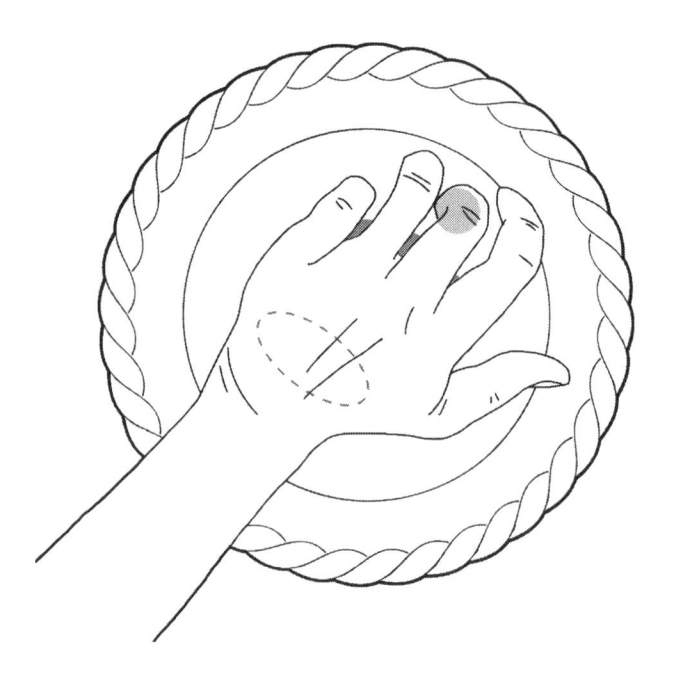

Gi notation

A solid notehead above the lower line

Gi strike

◌ Resting

● Strike area

TIP

Lift your elbow as you strike the drum. This will prevent your wrist from touching the drumhead and help to create a clearer tone.

Only the heel of your hand should dampen the drum.

PRACTICE PIECES

Practice Time   Play Along

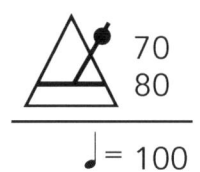

Gi Practice

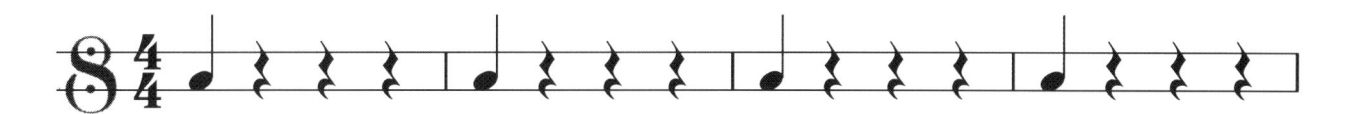

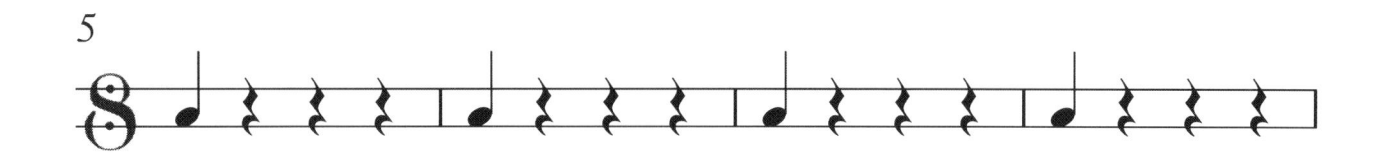

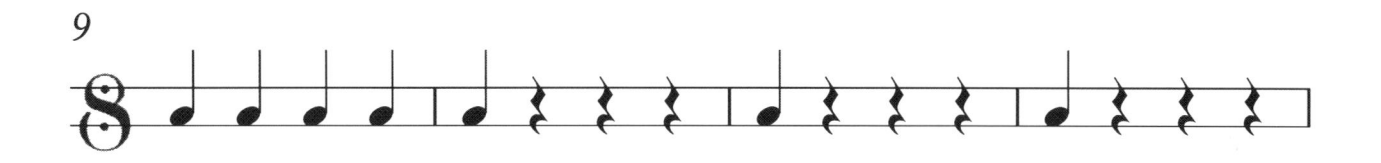

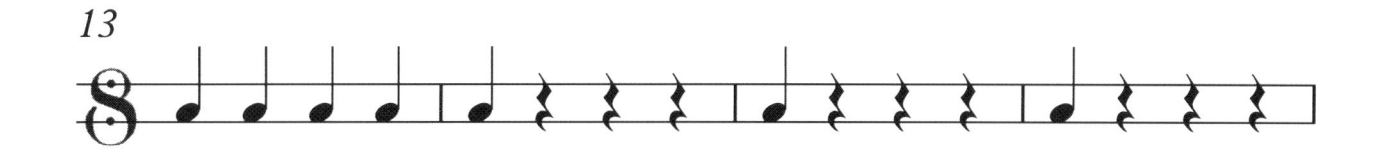

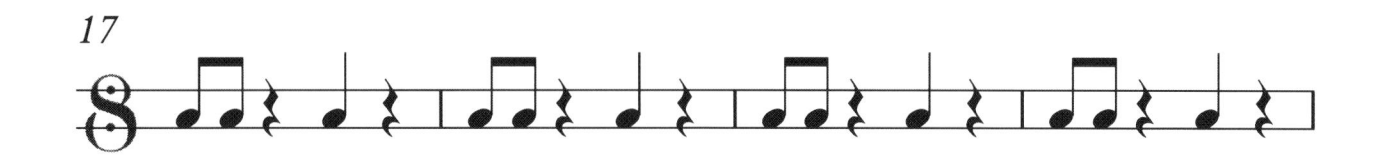

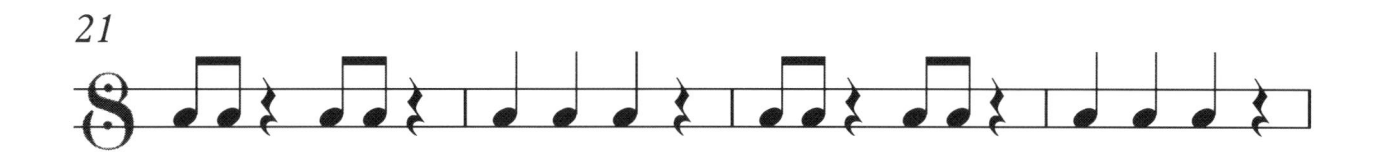

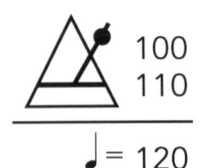

Gi Practice – with Ge

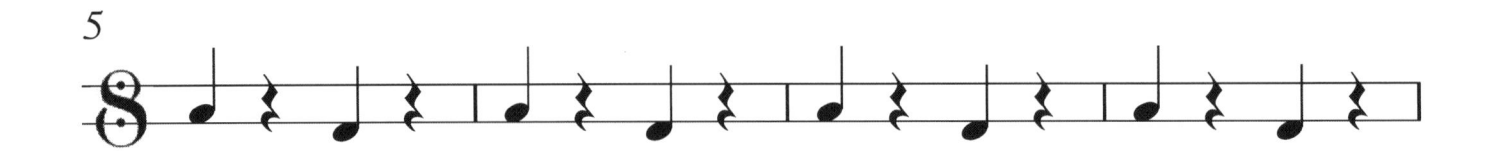

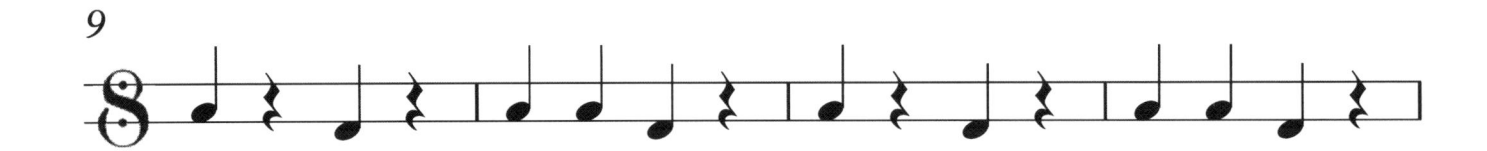

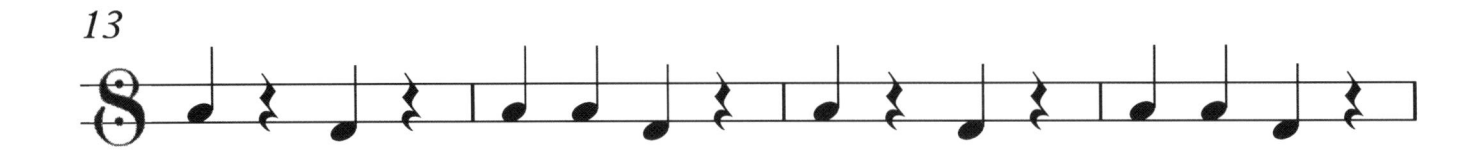

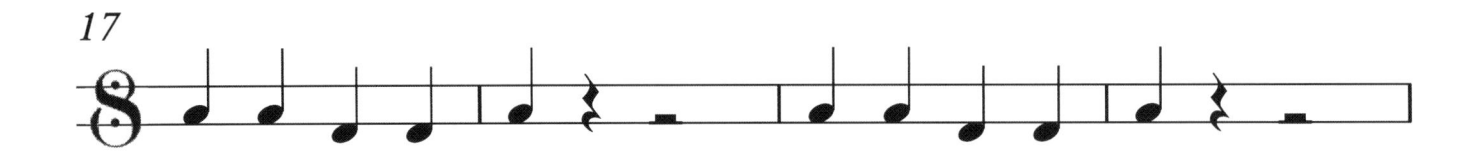

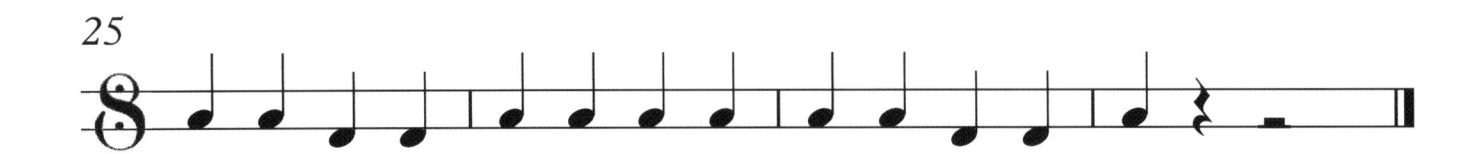

LARGE DRUM 13

Gi Practice – with Ge and Ke

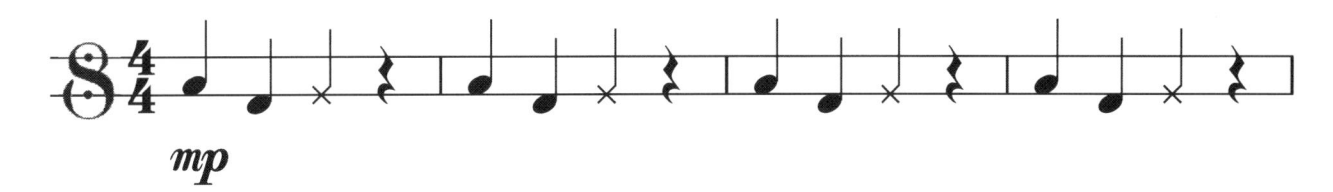

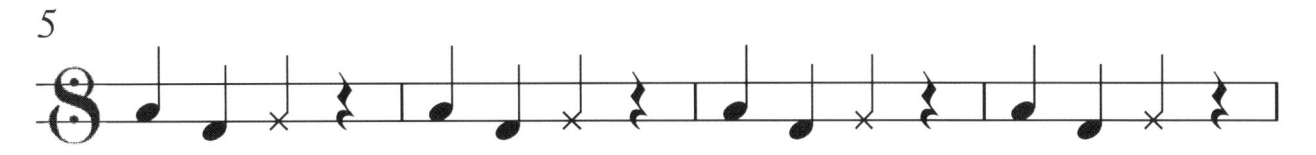

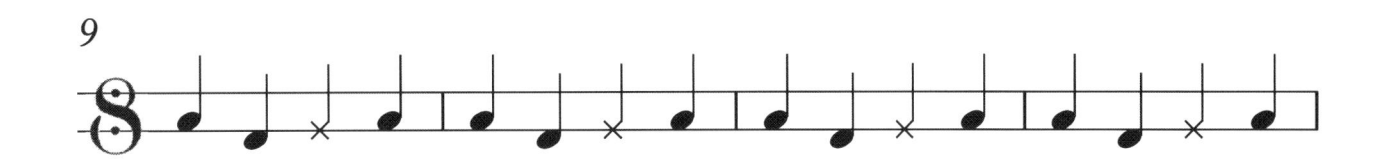

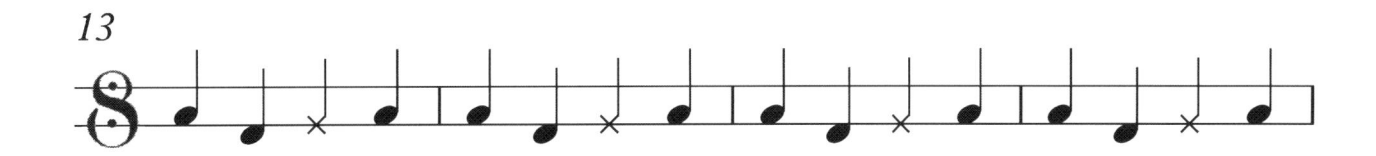

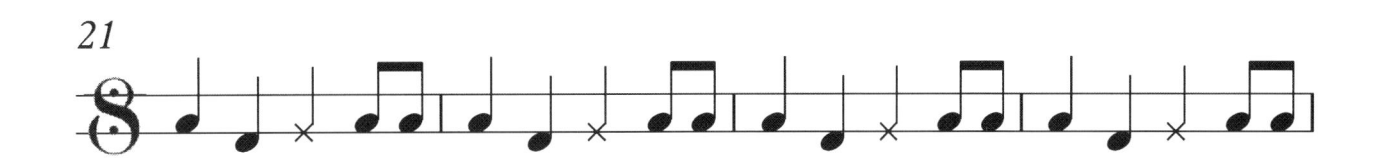

♩ = 60

Large Drum **Advanced Technique** Slide

The characteristic slide (also known as *Glissando*) is an iconic and instantly recognisable sound of the tabla.

It is commonly used to join the sound **Ge** to the sound **Gi**, but can also be used with the sound **Ga**.

When used as part of a rhythmical pattern, the glide helps to give the pattern its unique *personality* by adding a *pitch bend* to certain beats.

When playing the tabla drum in popular music or in a dance groove, it can be effective to slide the last beat in the pattern. The resulting effect is a natural feeling of *release* on the first beat of the cycle. This dynamic will become clear as you play the practice pieces on the following pages.

Follow these steps to play the **Ge** to **Gi** slide:

• Adopt the *resting position*.

• Play **Ge** and while the drum is still sounding, bring your hand back and place its heel on the edge of the drum close to you.

• Lift your elbow and whilst applying pressure to the drum with the heel of your hand, slide it towards the black spot.

• The resulting sound should be a clear-sounding *Doowoop*!

Ge to Gi slide

> *TIP*
>
> *Only the heel of your hand must touch the drum. Lifting your elbow as you slide will prevent your wrist from dampening the sound.*
>
> *Try experimenting by applying varying degrees of pressure until you get the desired effect.*

LARGE DRUM

Types of Slide

There are three main ways of creating slides.

Slide 1 **with resriking**

- Strike *Ge* (or *Ga*)
- Slide in the rhythm shown
- Restrike at *Gi*

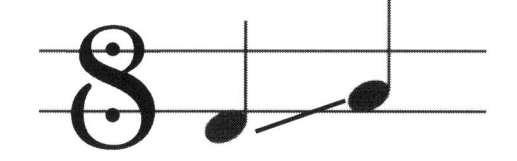

Slide 2 **without resriking**

- Strike *Ge* (or *Ga*)
- Slide in the rhythm shown
- Do not restrike at *Gi*

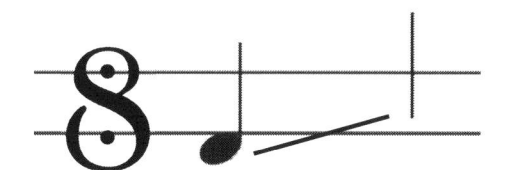

Slide 3 **combined strike and slide**

- Strike *Ge* whilst sliding
- The slide forms part of the note value and is not an *after-effect* like Slides 1 and 2
- The slide should make a *Woop* sound

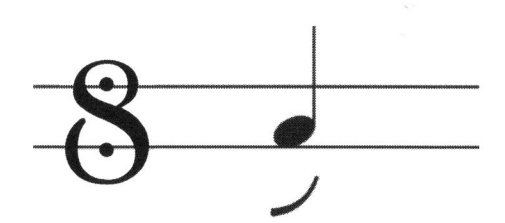

PRACTICE PIECES

On the following pages are six exercises for you to practise your slide techniques.

Practice Time   **Play Along**

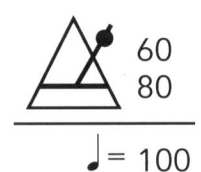

Slide 1 Practice

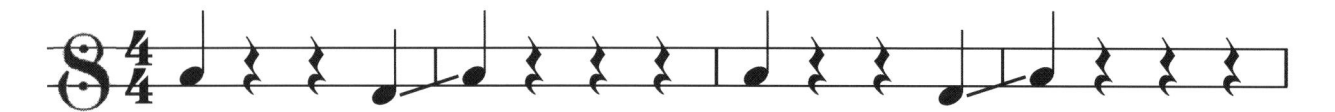

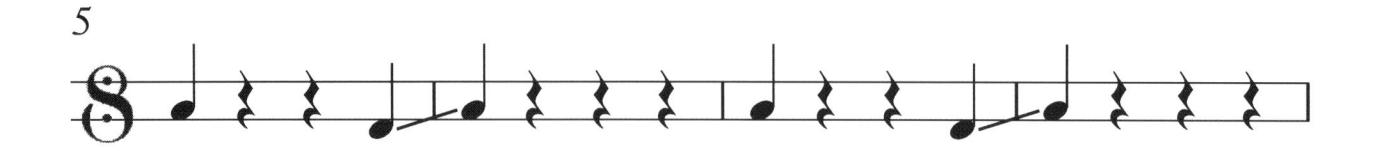

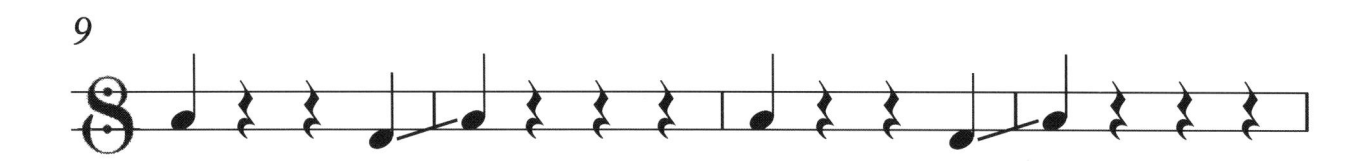

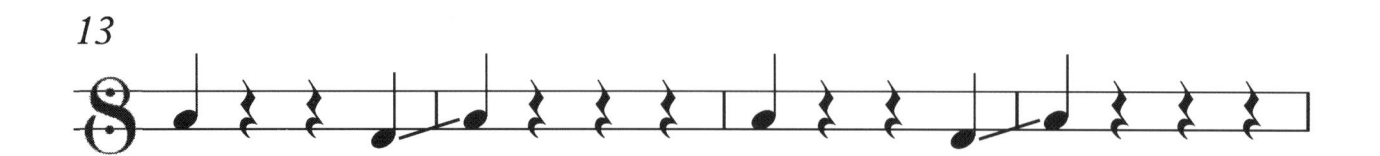

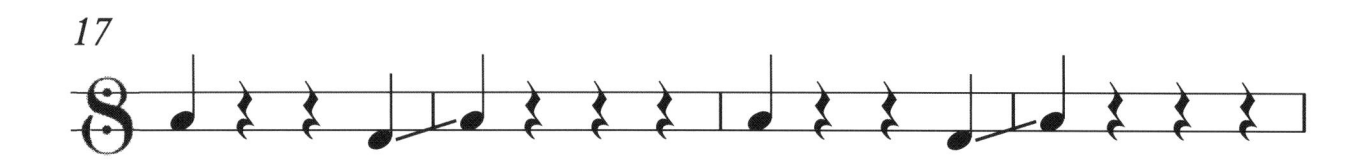

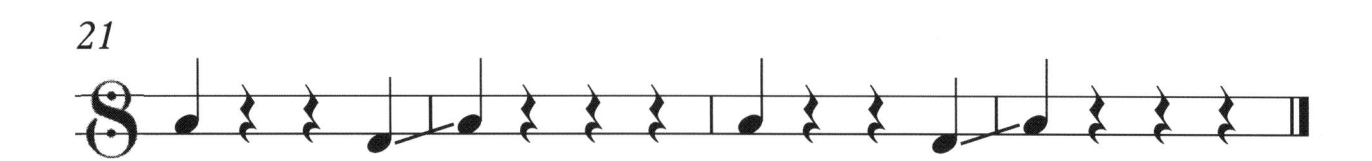

LARGE DRUM 17

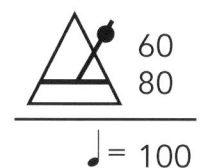

Slide 2 Practice

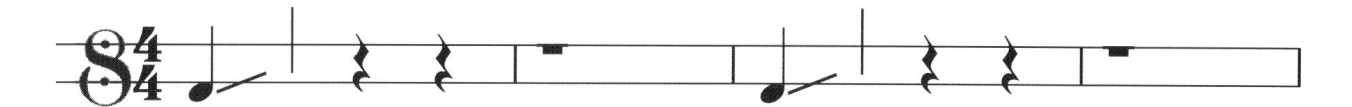

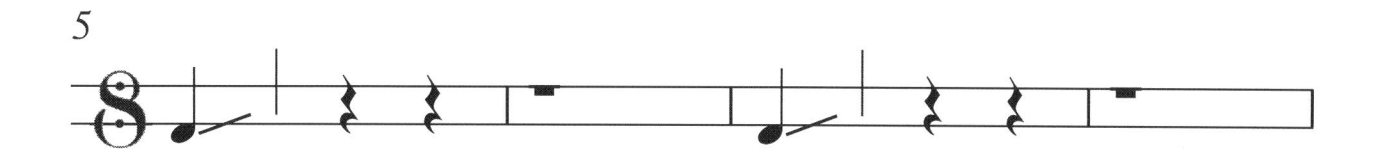

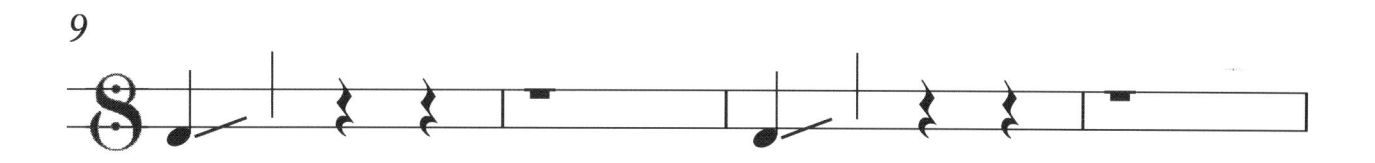

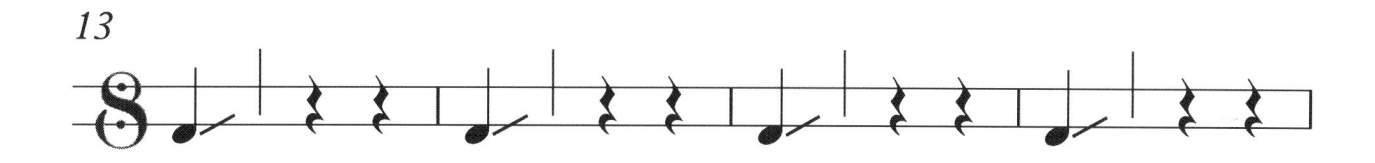

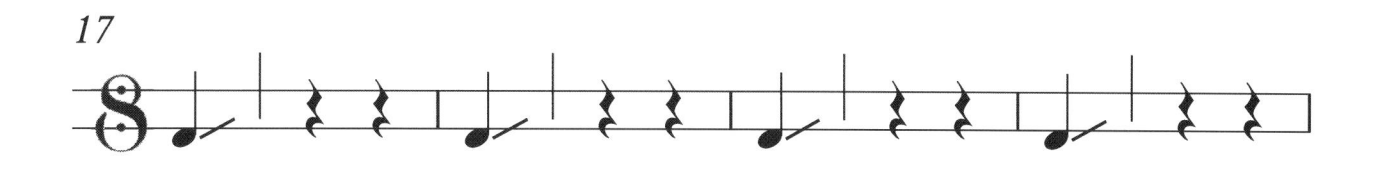

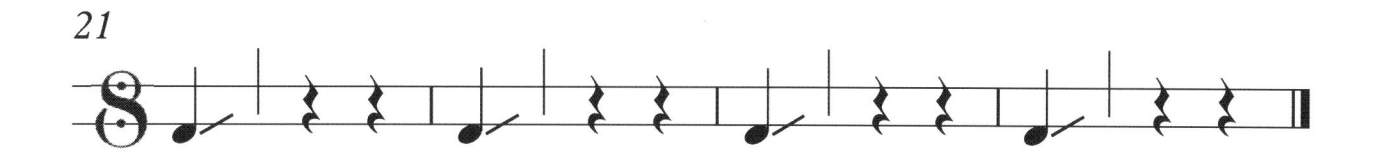

♩ = 100

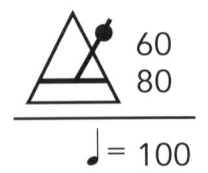

Slide 3 Practice

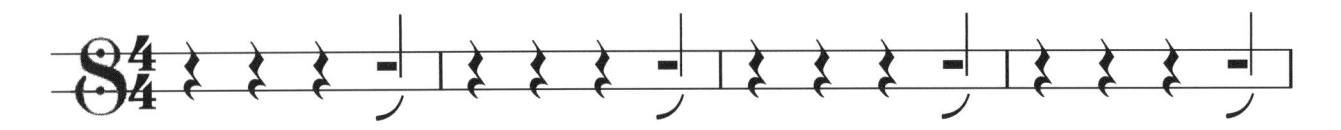

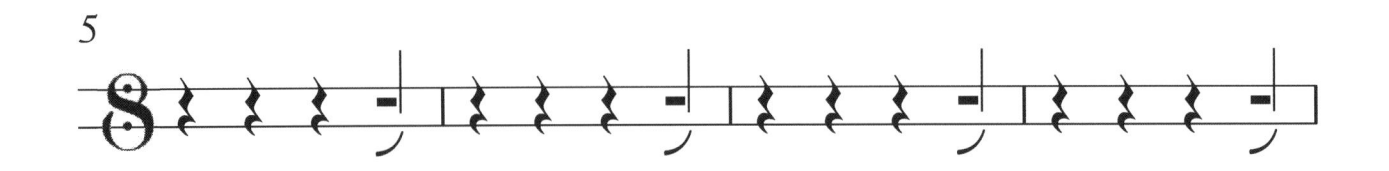

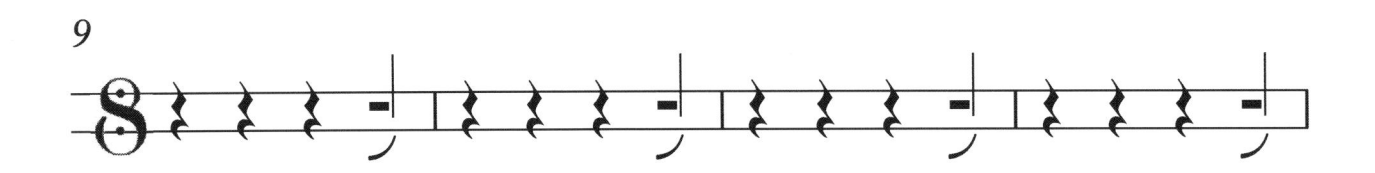

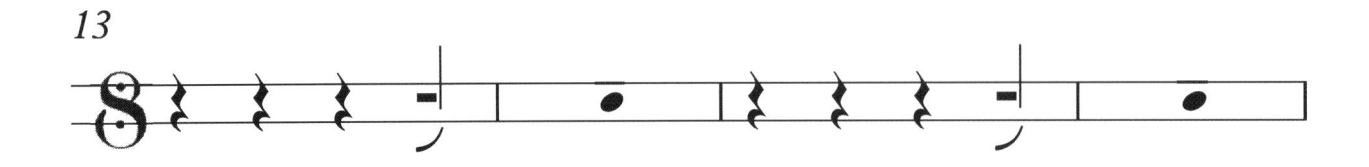

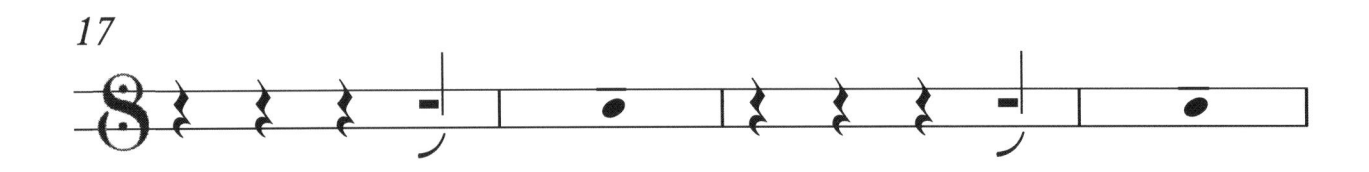

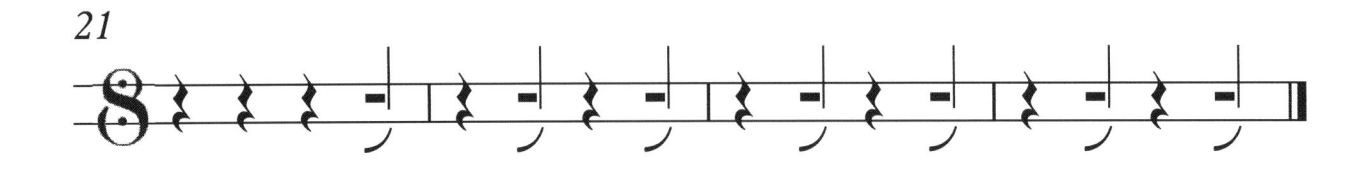

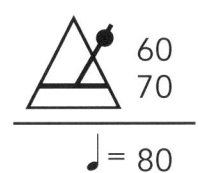

Ga Slide Practice

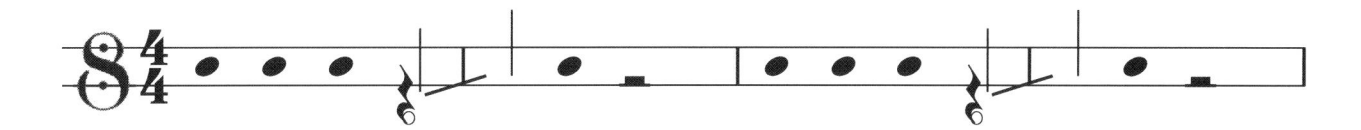

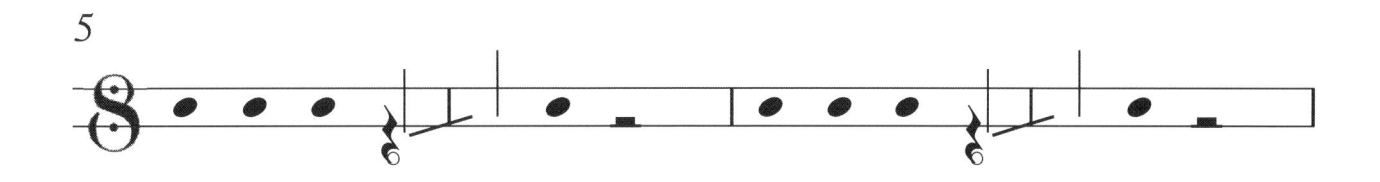

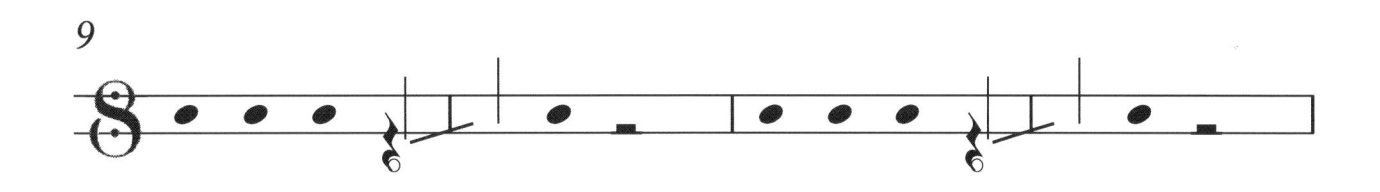

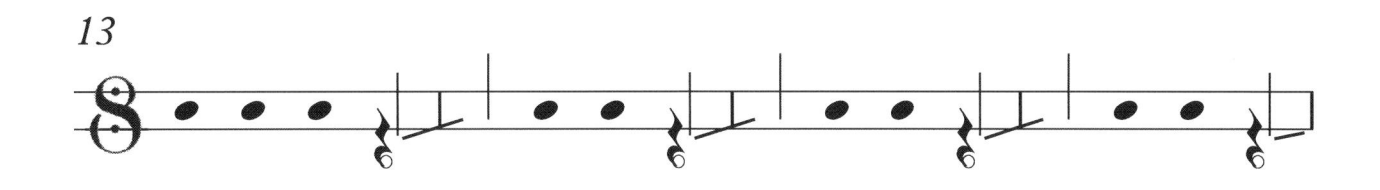

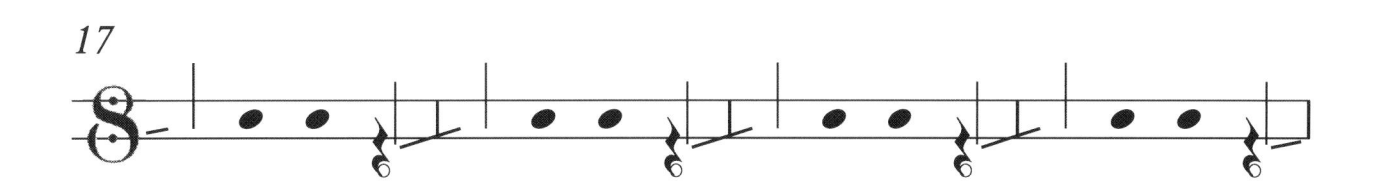

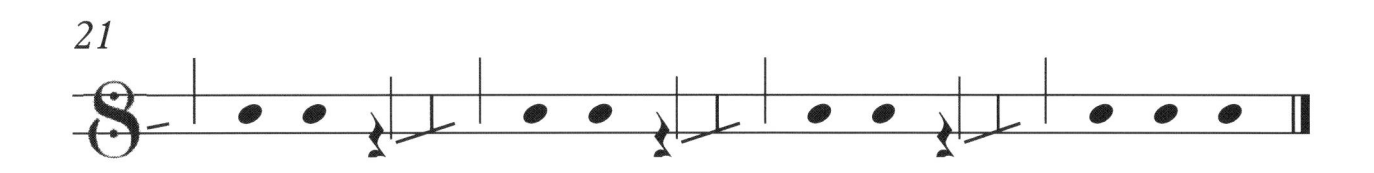

♩ = 80

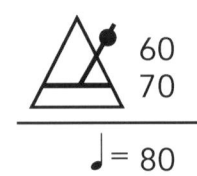

Three Slides Practice

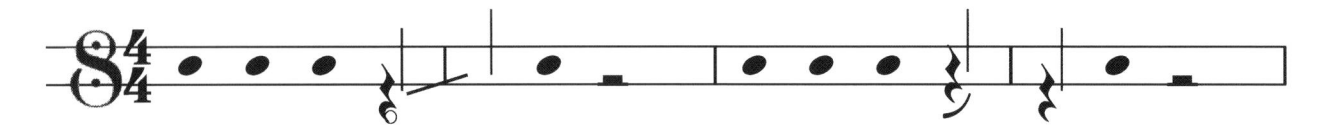

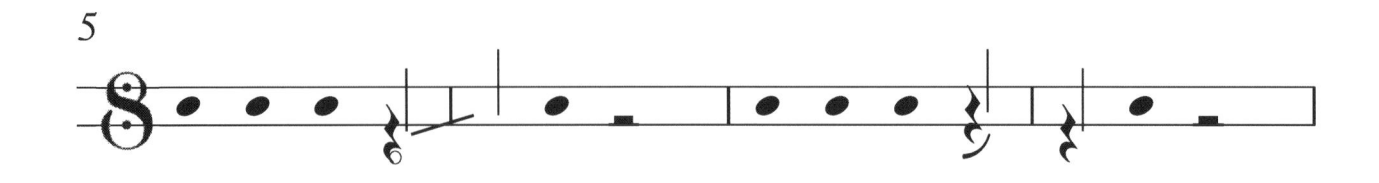

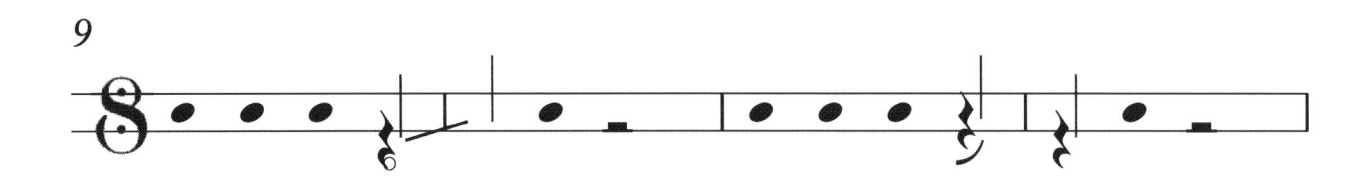

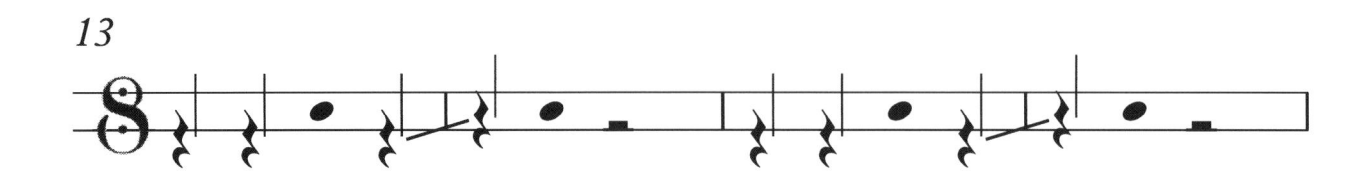

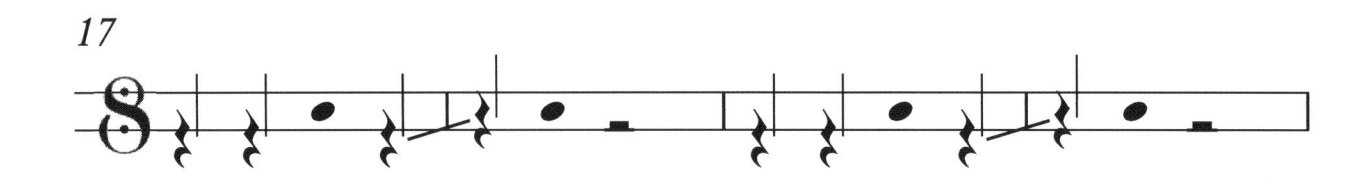

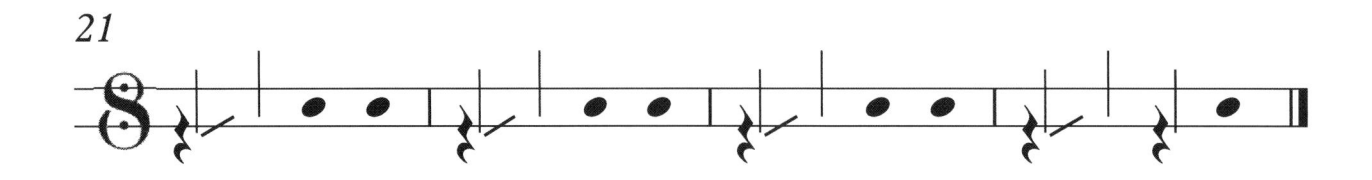

♩ = 80

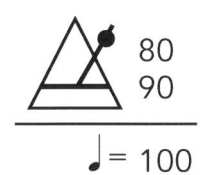

Dotted-Rhythm Slide Practice

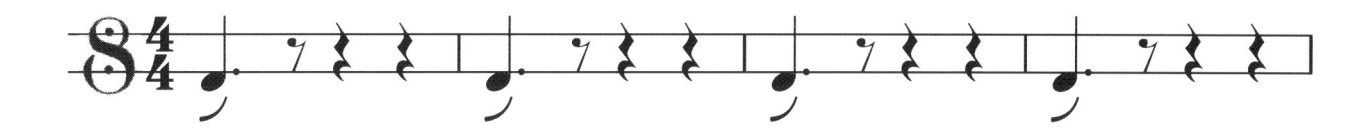

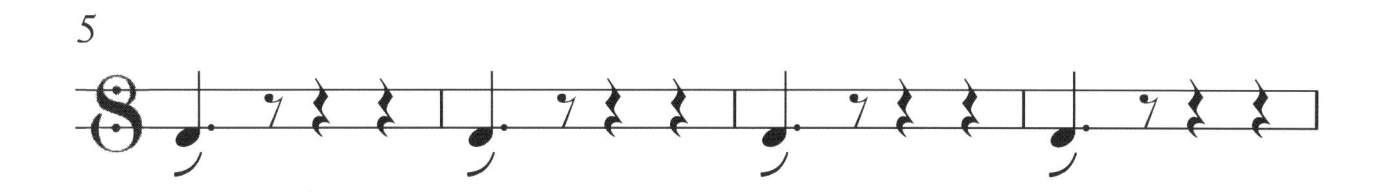

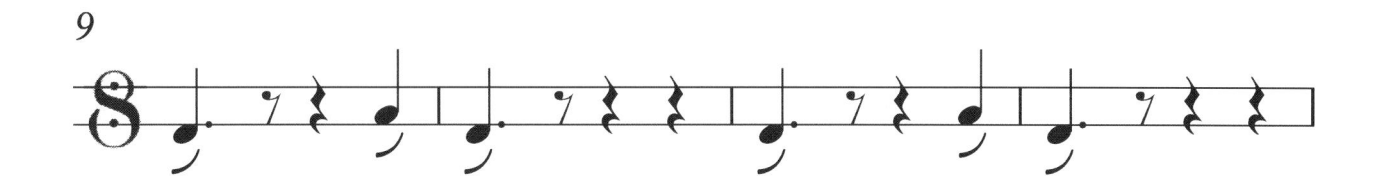

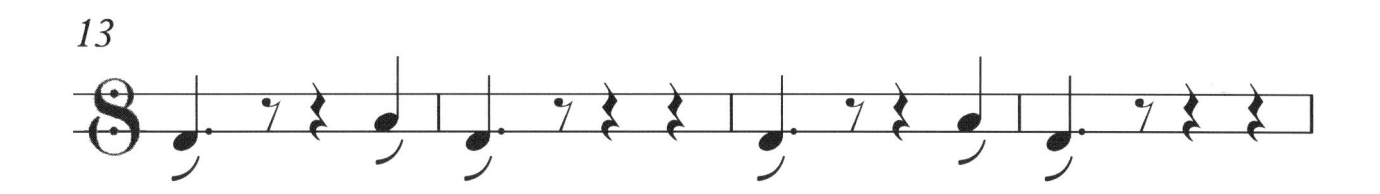

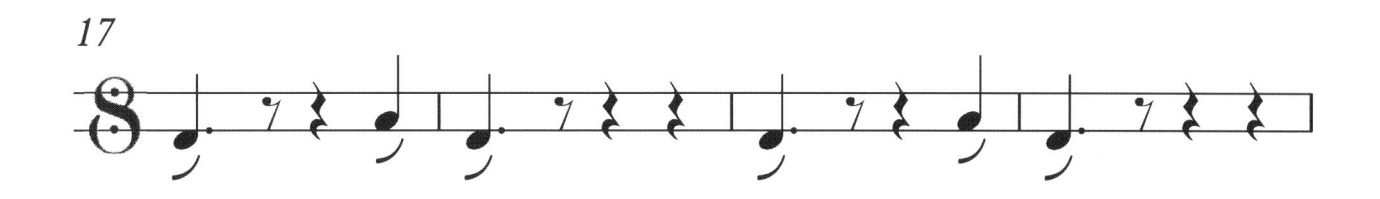

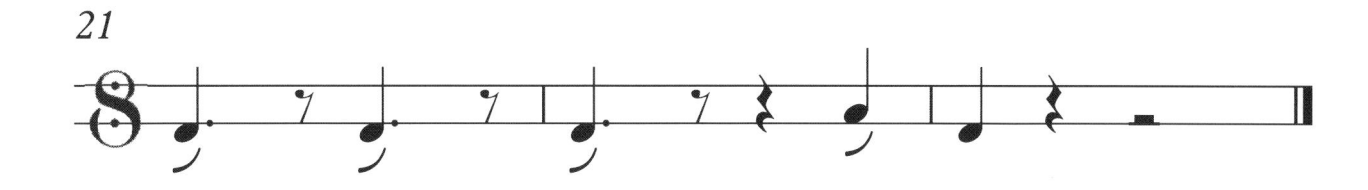

SMALLER DRUM

Smaller Drum **Muted Open Sound** Ta

Ta (pronounced *Tar*) is a dampened open sound played on the smaller drum. It can be considered to be a muted version of *Na*.

Follow these steps to play *Ta*:

• Adopt the *resting position*.

• Whilst keeping your fourth and fifth fingers in place, pivot your wrist away from you to gather momentum and then rotate your wrist back with a flicking motion to force your index finger to strike the drum. It should land close to the edge of the black spot.

• The top two joints of your index finger should strike the drum – not just the tip. This can only be achieved by keeping your finger straight and rigid whilst striking.

• The movement is very similar to that used in *Na*, but with your index finger striking the drum close to the black spot instead of the edge.

• The tonal quality of *Ta* is duller than that of Na and not as crisp-sounding. This difference in timbre is more noticeable when the two sounds are played one after the other.

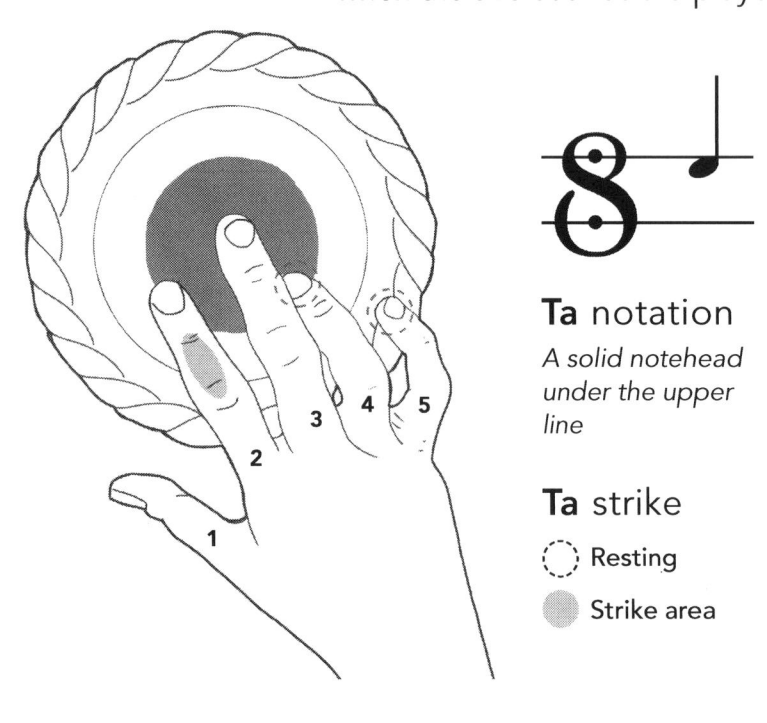

Ta notation
A solid notehead under the upper line

Ta strike
◌ Resting
● Strike area

PRACTICE PIECES

Practice Time   **Play Along**

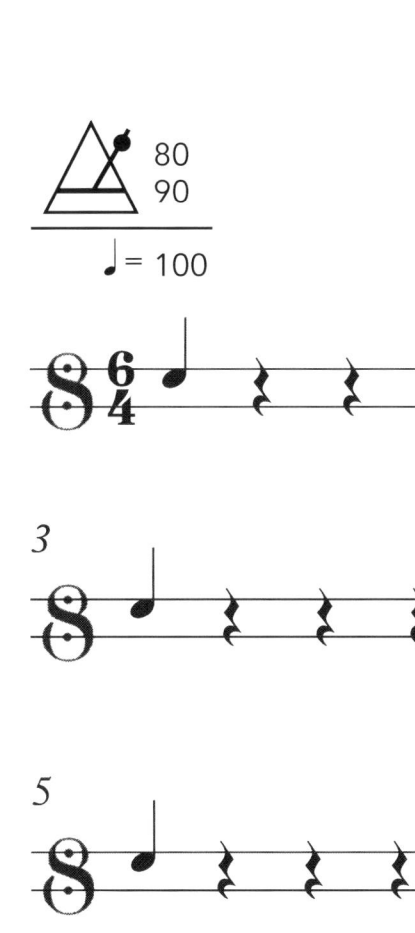

Ta Practice

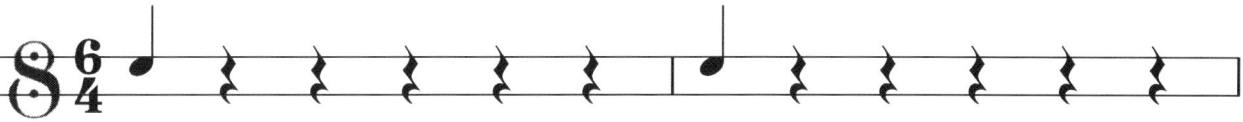

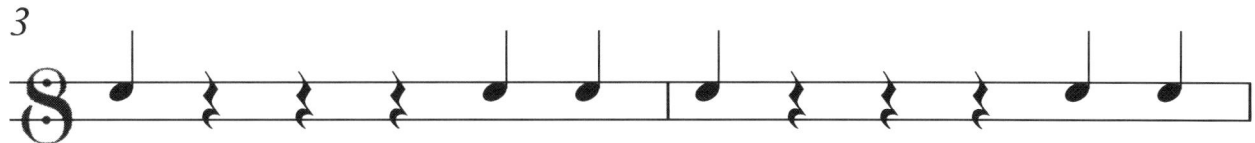

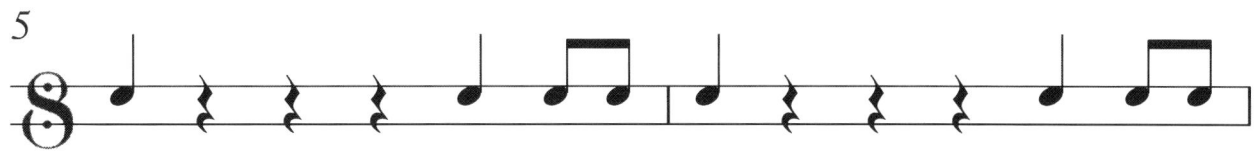

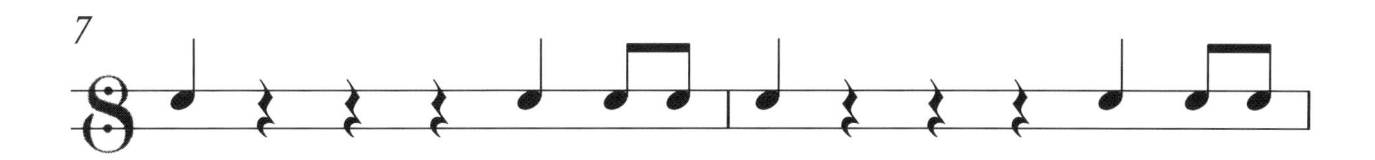

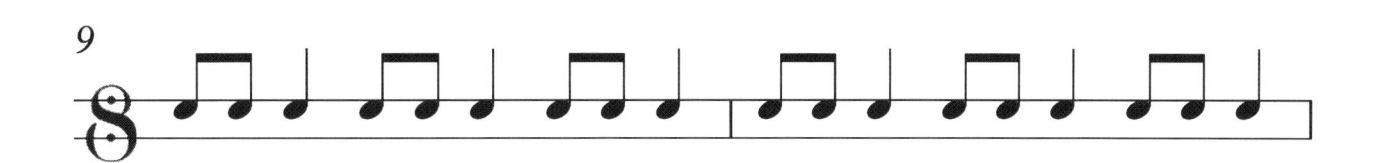

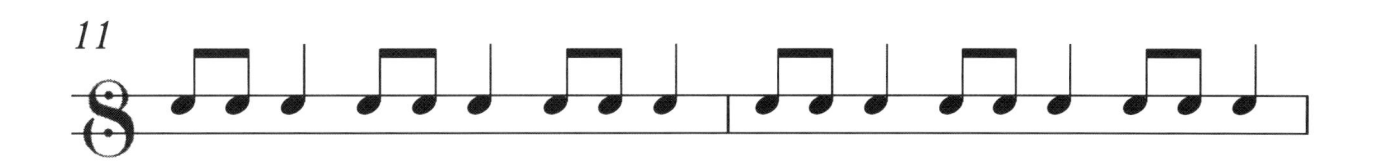

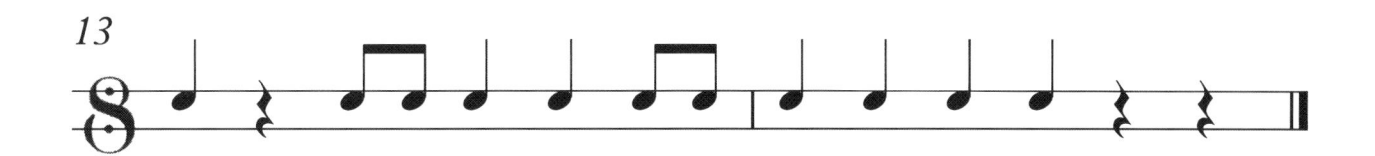

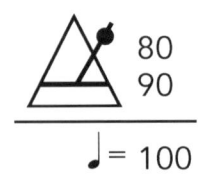

Ta Practice – with Na

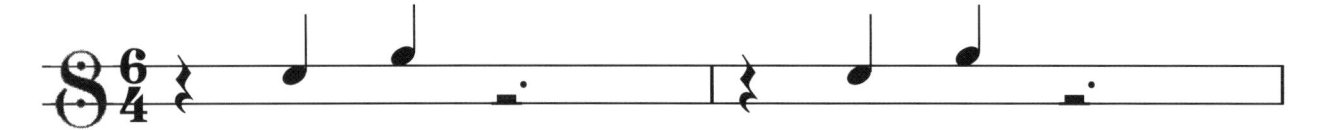

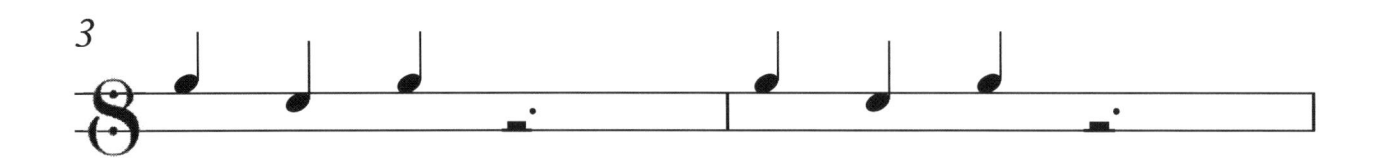

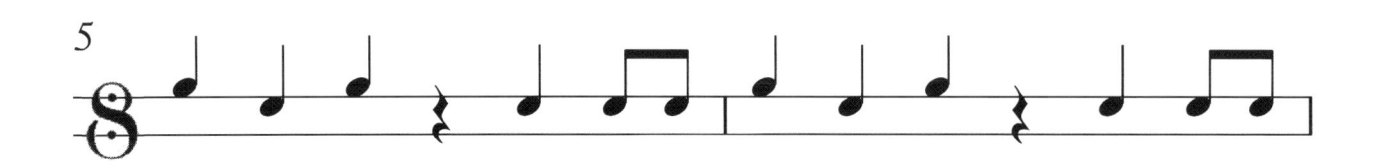

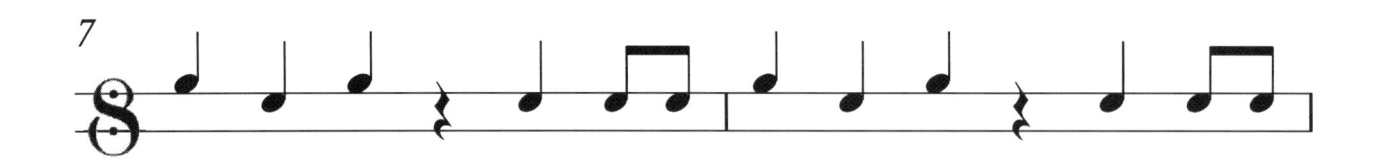

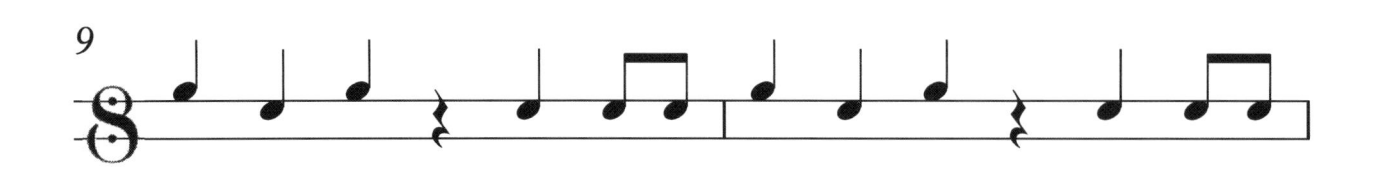

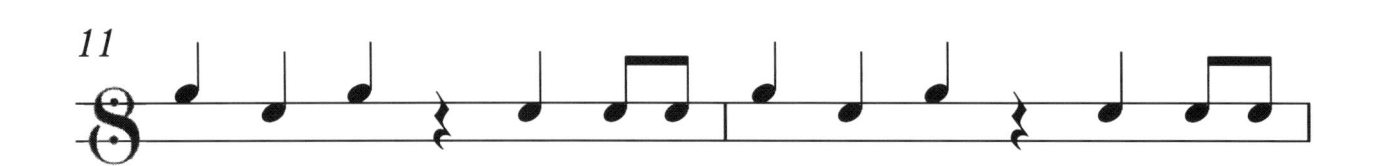

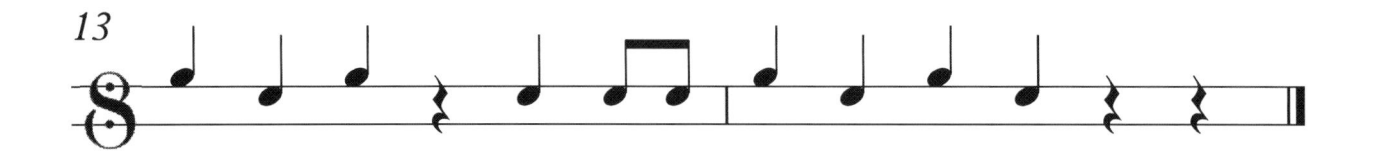

Ta Practice – with Na and Te

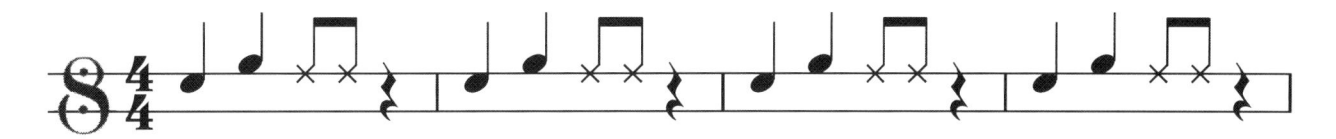

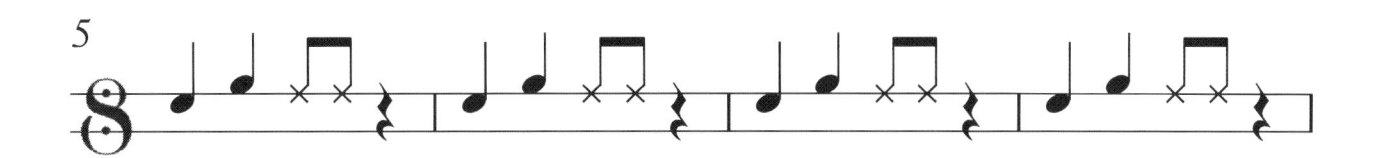

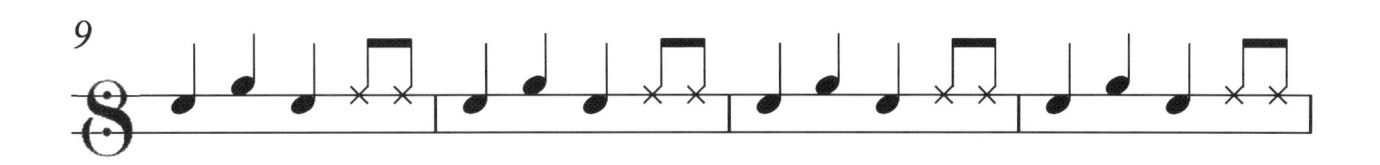

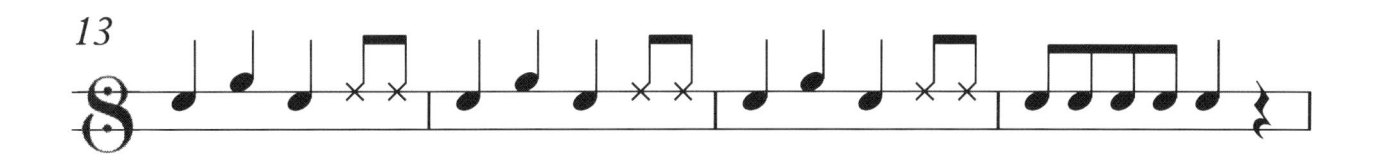

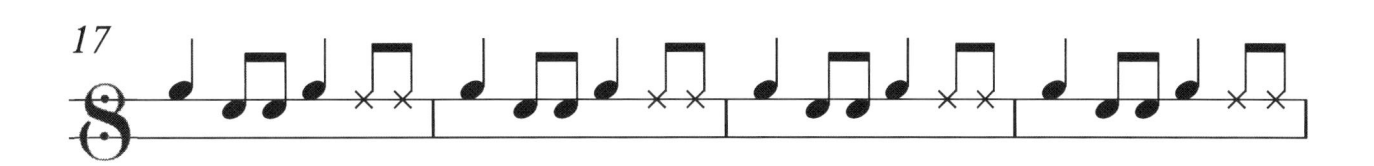

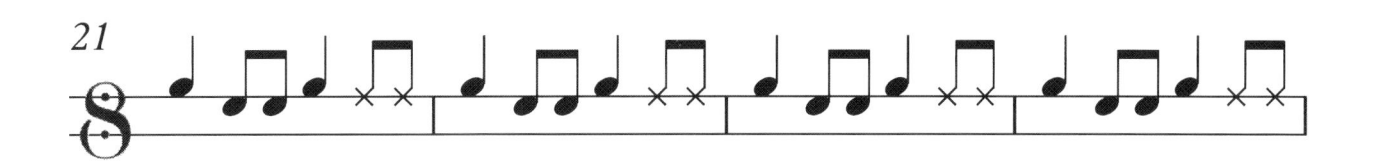

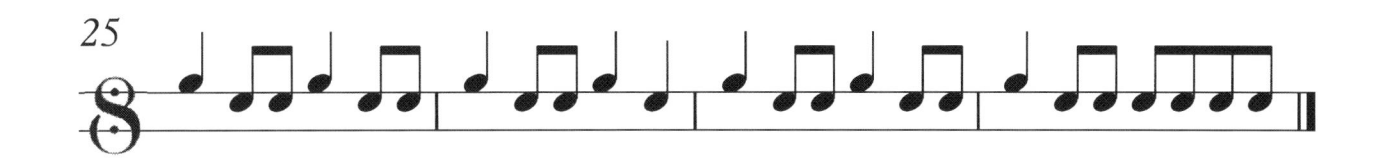

Smaller Drum
Advanced Technique – Closed Sound **Ti**

The most commonly used closed sound on the smaller tabla drum is *Te*. However, it is also possible to create another type of closed sound *Ti*, which has a different quality of tone and timbre.

Ti is created by striking the drum in a very similar manner to the *Na* strike. However, the third finger is placed on the black spot before the strike – thus preventing any resonance.

Ti is a dry, clicky sound created on the edge of the drum. It is sharper and brighter than *Te* and very effective when played in a groove or dance pattern.

To play the sound *Ti*:

- Adopt the *resting position* with your fourth and fifth fingers in place.

- Place the tip of your middle finger onto the black spot.

- Strike the drum on the edge as if performing the stroke for *Na*, but while keeping your middle finger on the black spot to prevent any resonance.

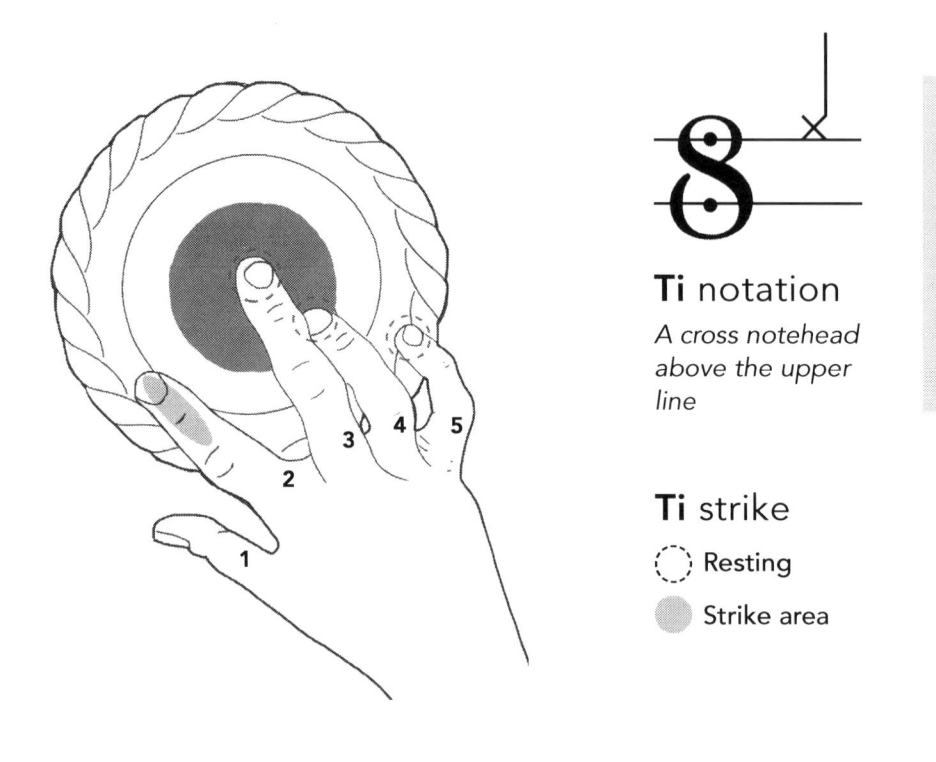

Ti notation

A cross notehead above the upper line

TIP

*Hold your index finger down after the strike – as if it had **stuck** to the drumhead. This will ensure that the resulting sound is fully muted.*

Ti strike

◌ Resting

● Strike area

PRACTICE PIECE

Practice Time   **Play Along**

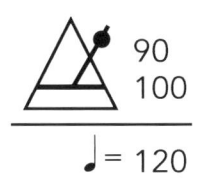

Ti Practice – with Na

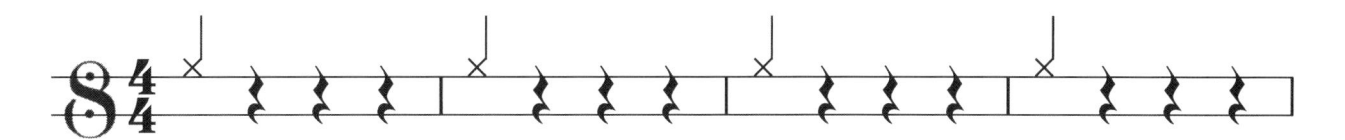

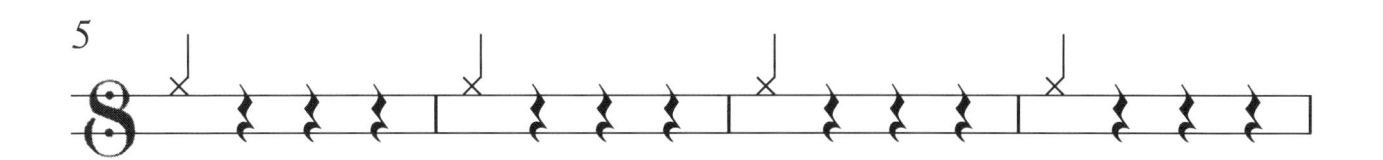

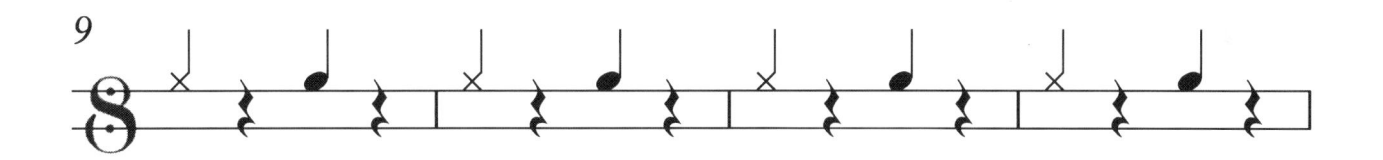

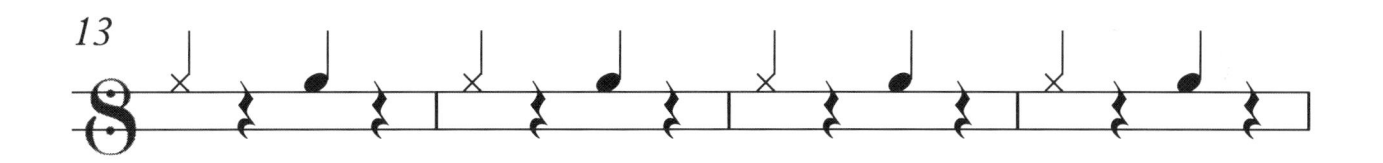

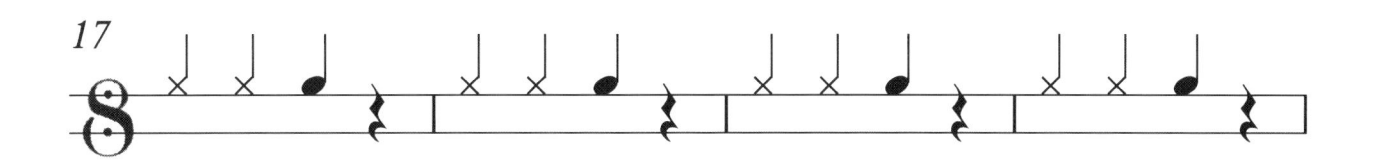

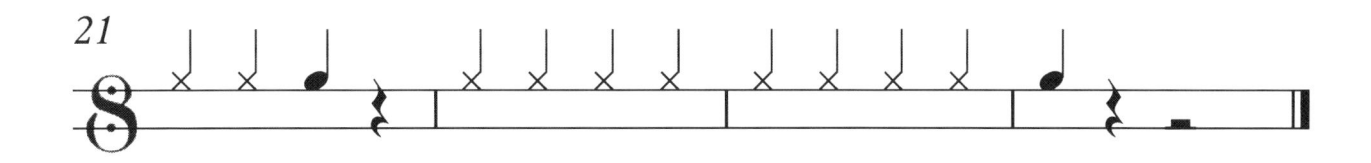

BOTH DRUMS – COMBINED SOUNDS

There are over twenty sounds that can be created by striking both drums simultaneously.

In this section, we will study the two most commonly used sounds – *Da* and *Di*. Some of the other *combined sounds* can be found used within the Solo Pieces in this module.

ONLINE
Video demonstration
Learn & Support >
DrumWise

Combined Open Sound **Da**

Da is pronounced as in the word *dark* and is one of the most commonly-played sounds on the tabla.

It is frequently used to denote the downbeat and other accented beats within a rhythm pattern. This will become clearer as you study traditional *Taala* rhythms in Module 3.

Da is played by striking *Ge* on the large drum and *Na* on the smaller drum at the same time.

To play the sound *Da*:

- Adopt the *resting position*.
- Prepare to strike.
- Strike both drums at exactly the same time.

The resulting sound should be open, but gently muted.

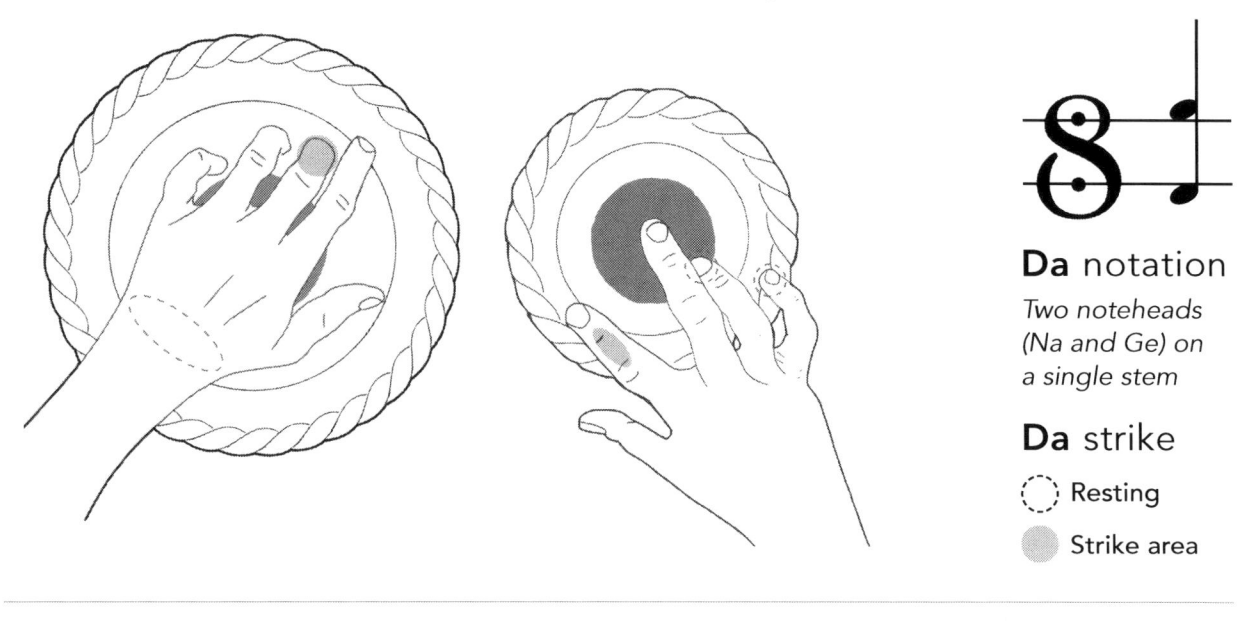

Da notation
Two noteheads (Na and Ge) on a single stem

Da strike
◌ Resting
● Strike area

PRACTICE PIECES

Practice Time   **Play Along**

Da Practice

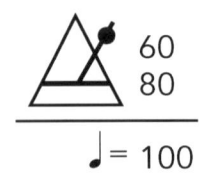

Da Practice –
with Slide, Ge and Na

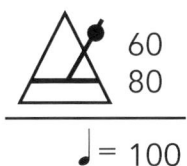

Da Practice –
with Slide, Ge, Tu and Na

Combined Open Sound **Di**

Di is pronounced as in the word *distant*.

It can be described as a muted version of the sound *Da* and is played by striking *Gi* on the large drum and *Ta* on the smaller drum at the same time.

To play the sound *Di*:

• Start with both hands in their **resting positions**.

• Prepare to strike.

• Strike both drums at exactly the same time.

The resulting sound should be open, but strongly dampened.

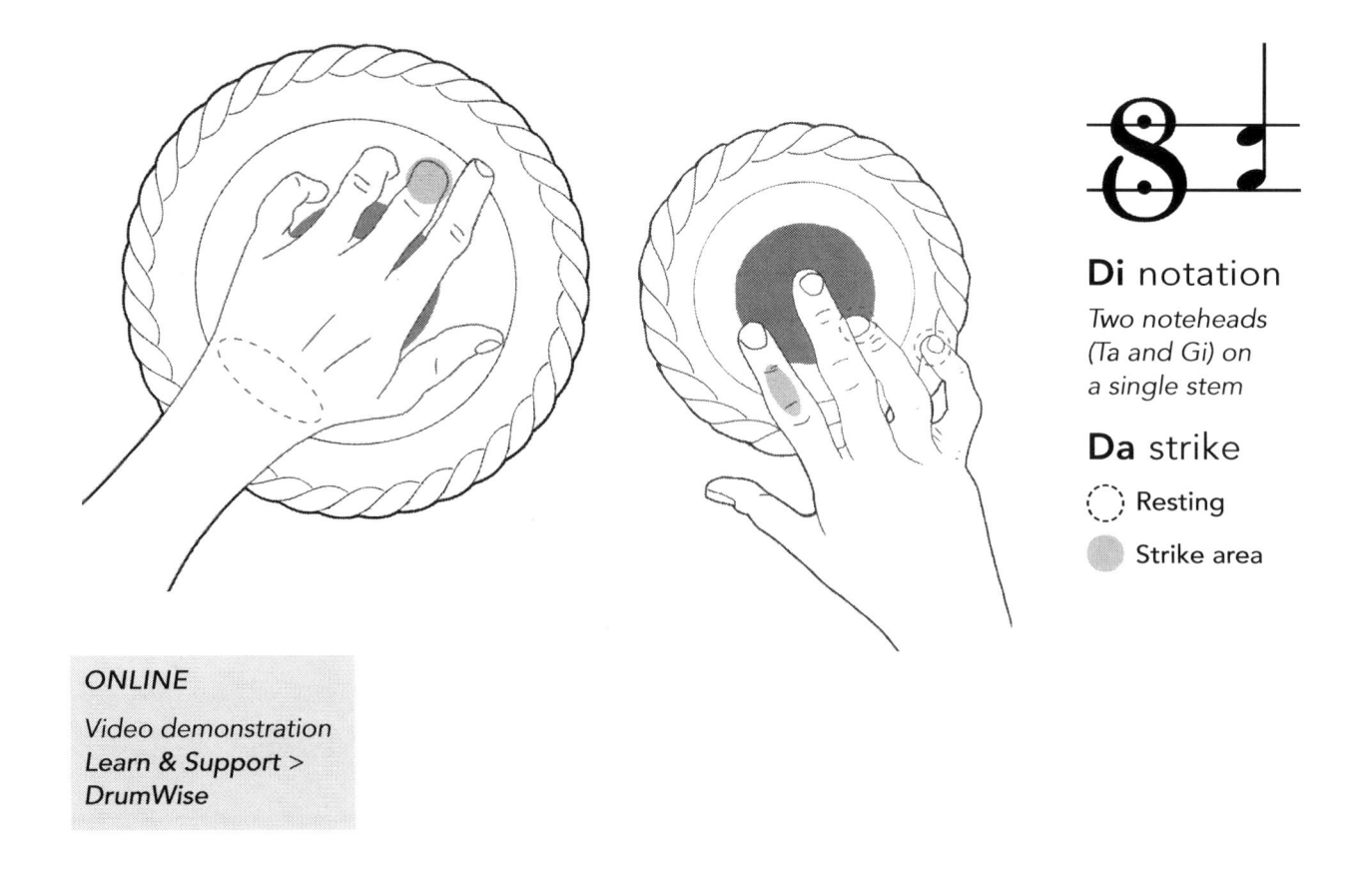

Di notation
Two noteheads (Ta and Gi) on a single stem

Da strike

◌ Resting

⬤ Strike area

ONLINE

Video demonstration
Learn & Support > DrumWise

PRACTICE PIECES

Practice Time   **Play Along**

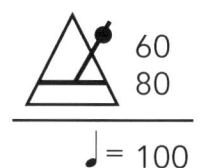

Di Practice

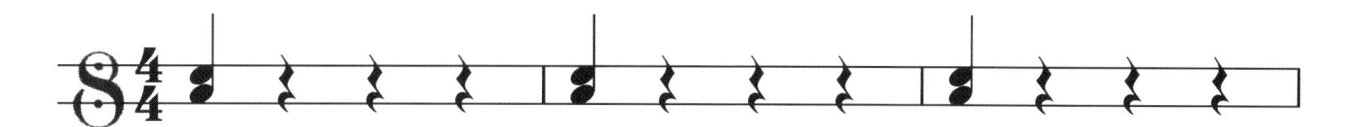

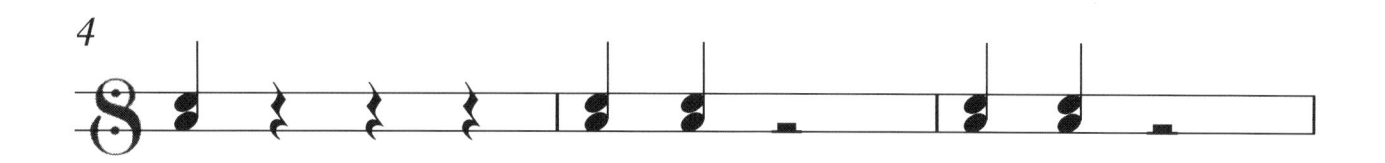

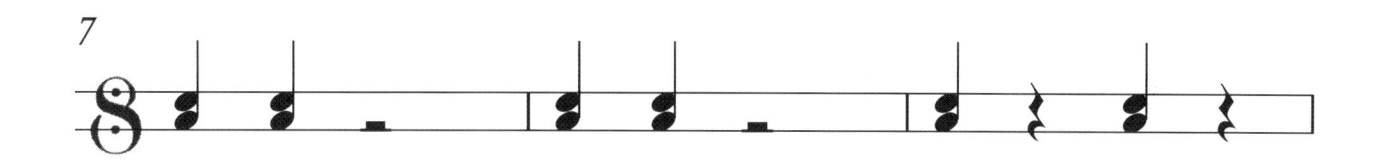

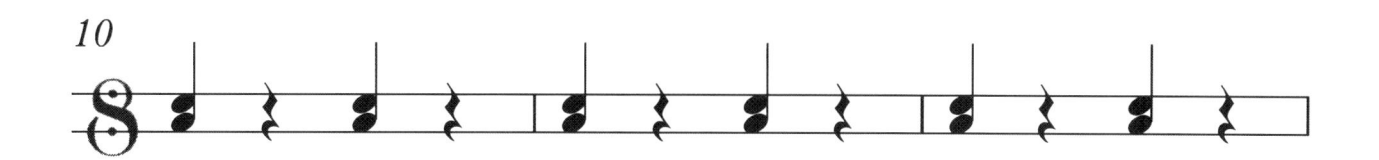

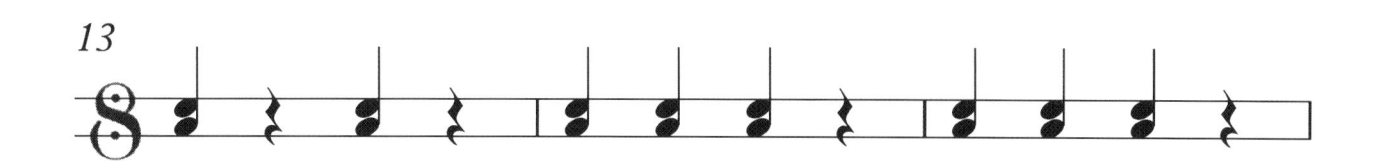

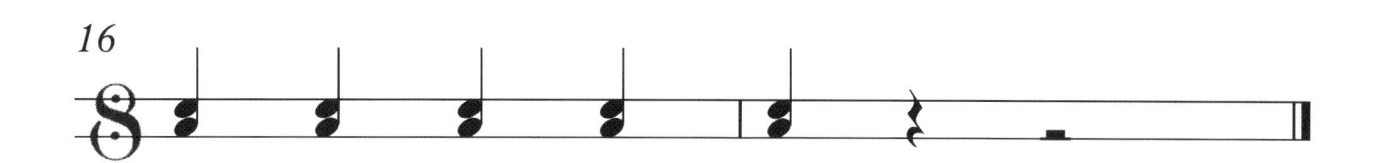

Di Practice –
with Slide and Da

Di Practice –
with Slide, **Da**, **Gi** and **Na**

SOLO PIECES

Well done on learning all of the basic sounds of the tabla drum!

The following solo pieces can be performed at your own preferred speed. However, practise slowly to start with using a metronome and the suggested tempos.

Play Along

Scores & Parts

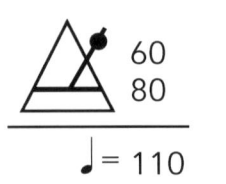

Tabla Solo 4

Kuljit Bhamra

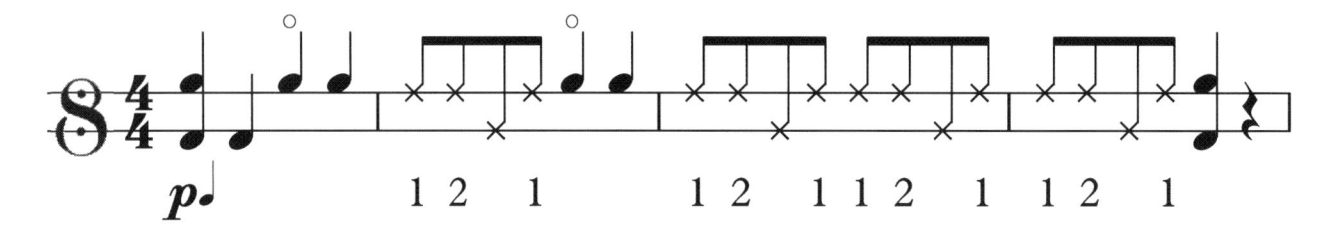

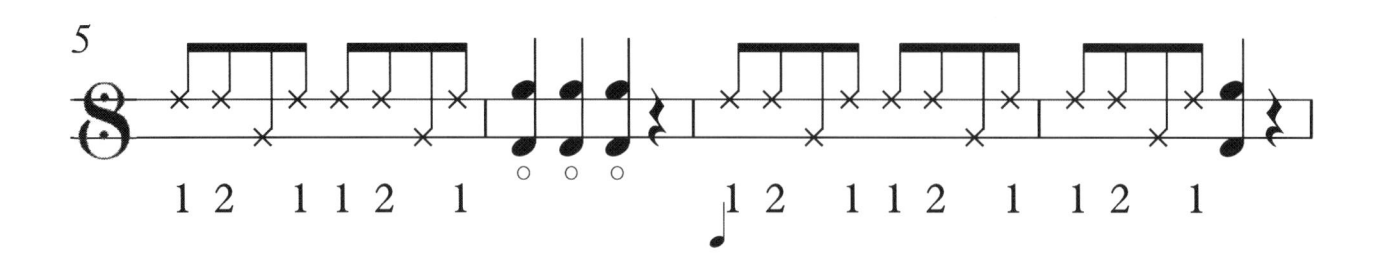

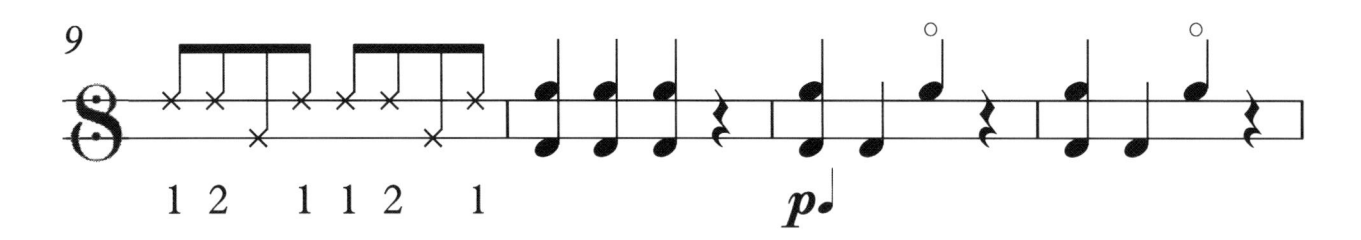

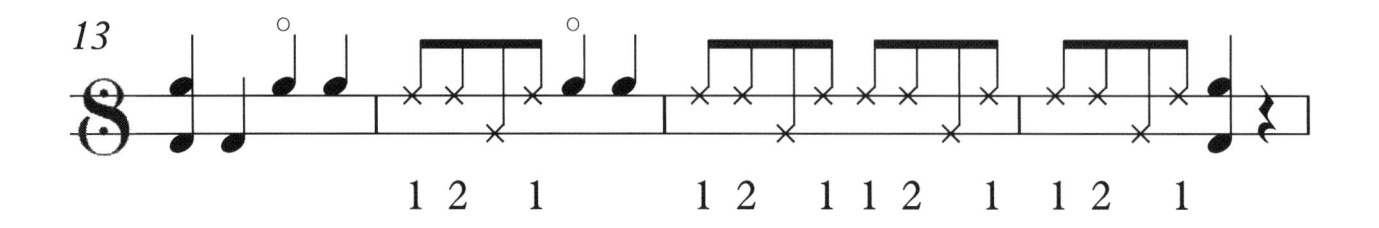

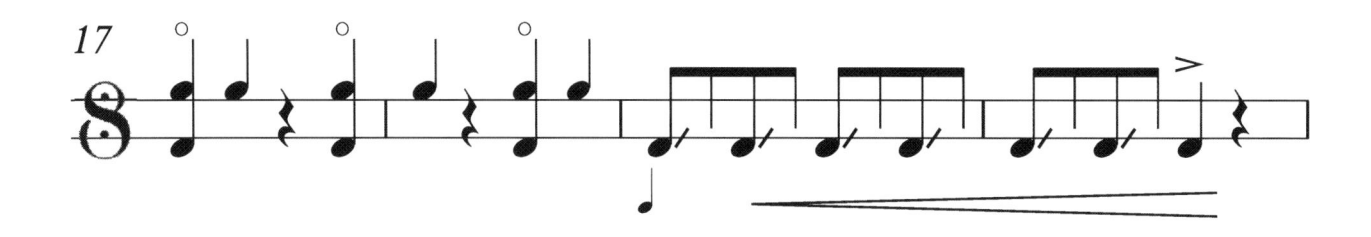

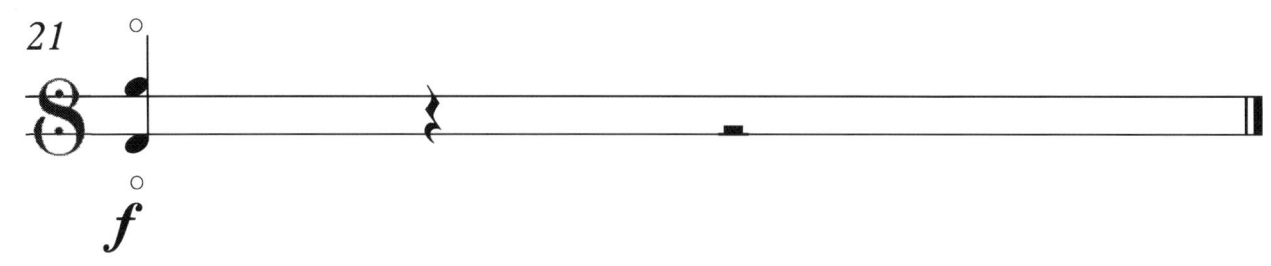

SOLO 39

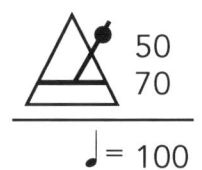

Tabla Solo 5

Kuljit Bhamra

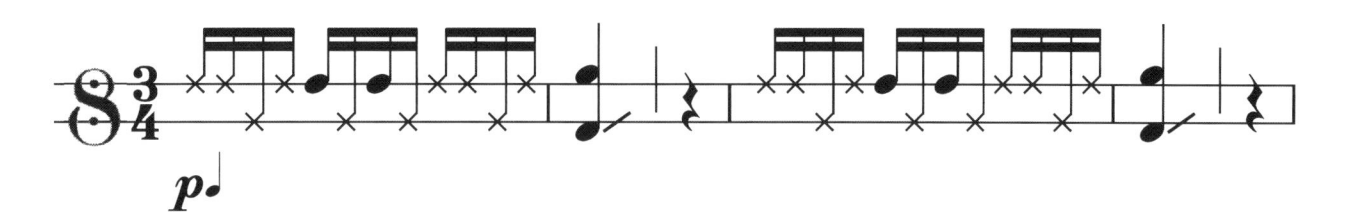

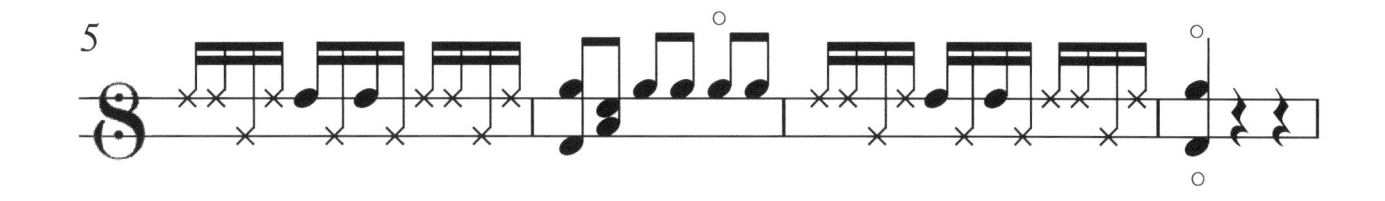

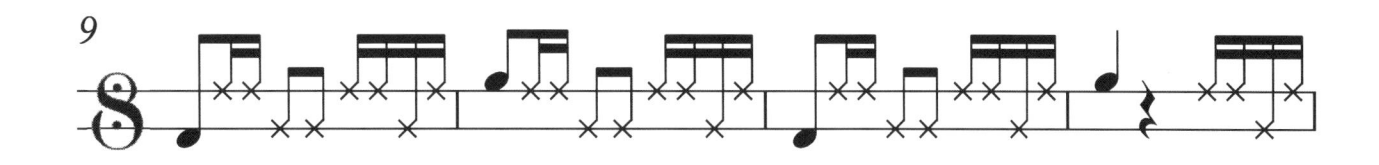

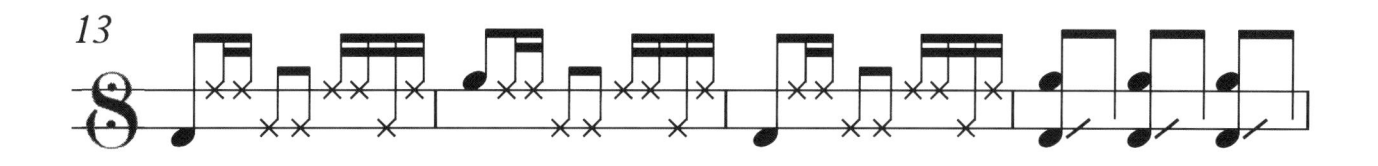

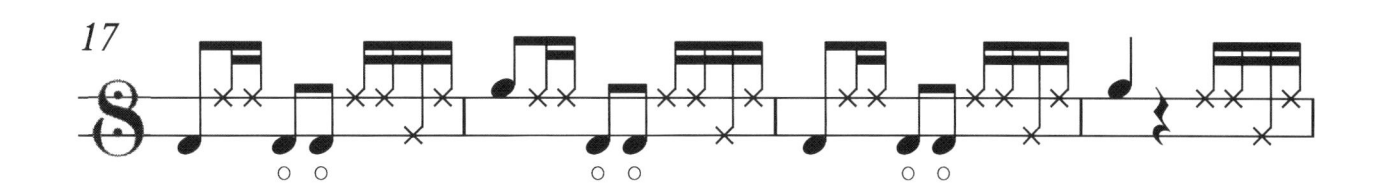

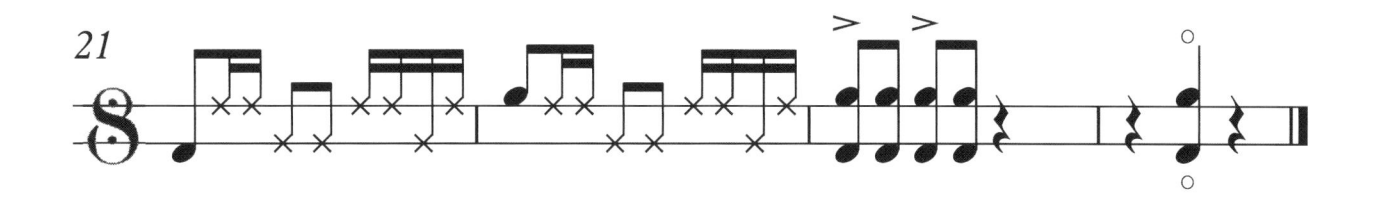

♩ = 100

40 MODULE 2

Tabla Solo 6

Kuljit Bhamra

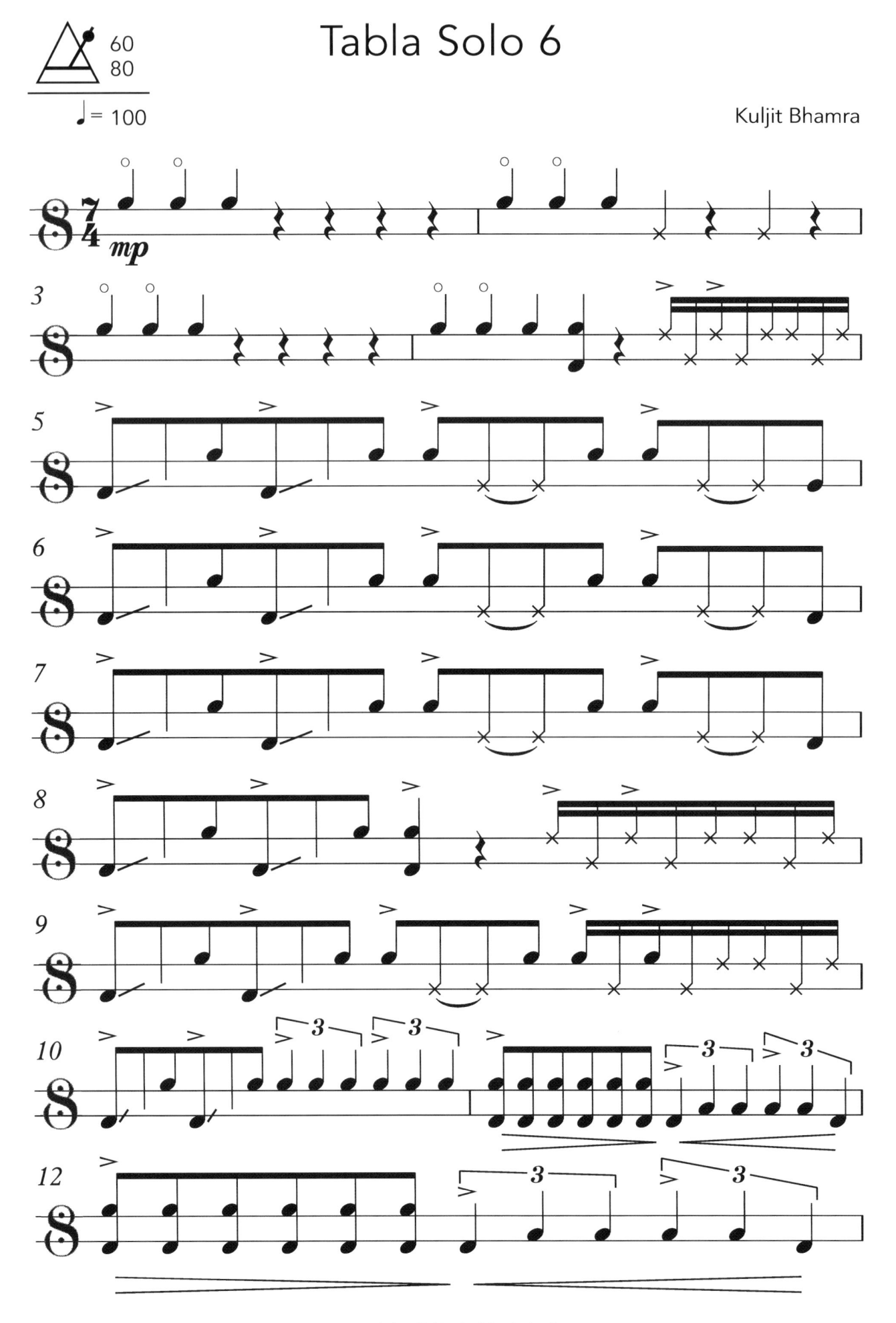

♩ = 100

SOLO 41

GROUP PIECES

In the following pieces, instruments can be added or replaced depending on what you have available in your classroom or college.

Play Along

Scores & Parts

Sheet Music
Purchase exciting new music online

Group Piece 5

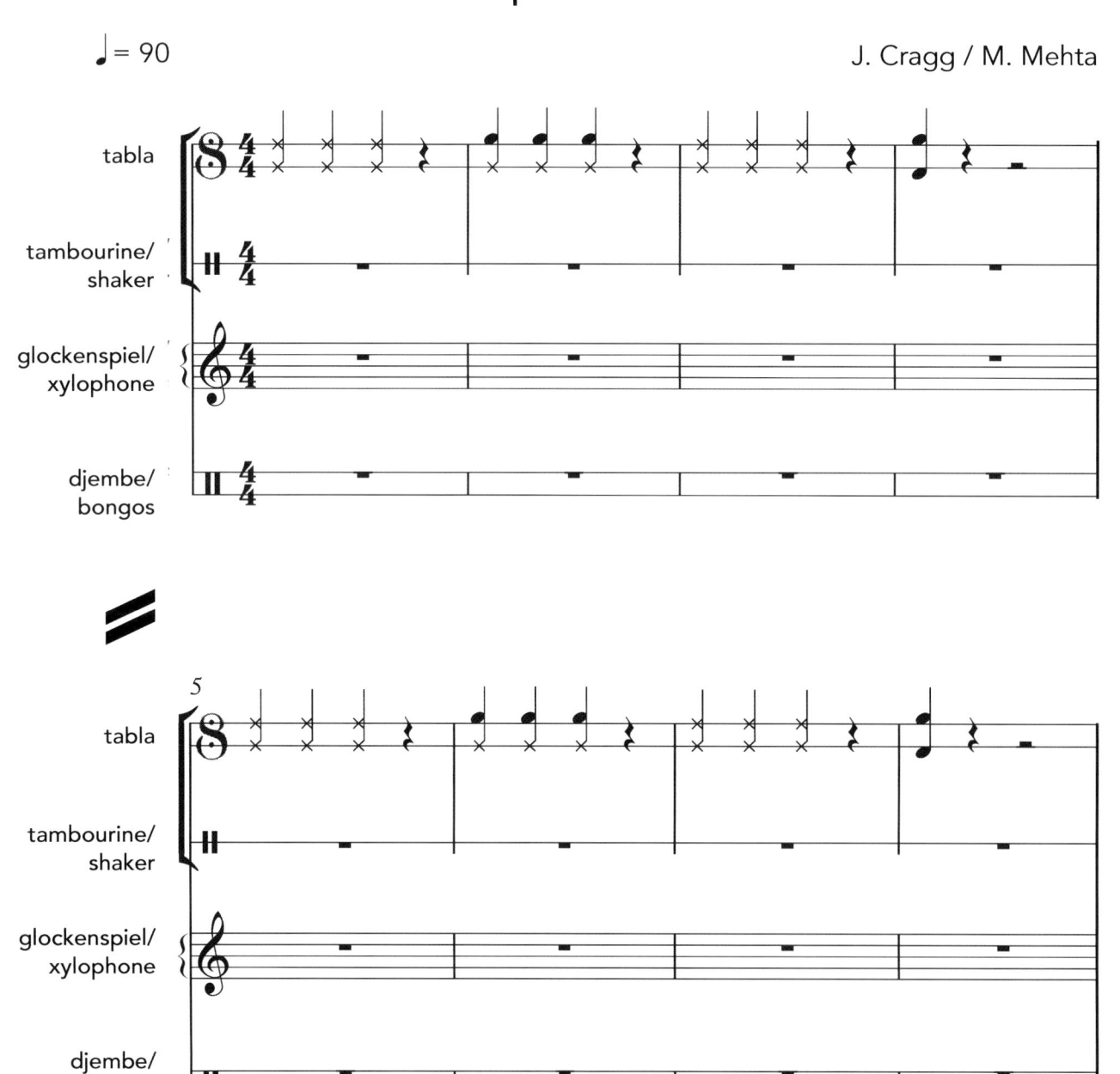

♩ = 90

J. Cragg / M. Mehta

GROUP 45

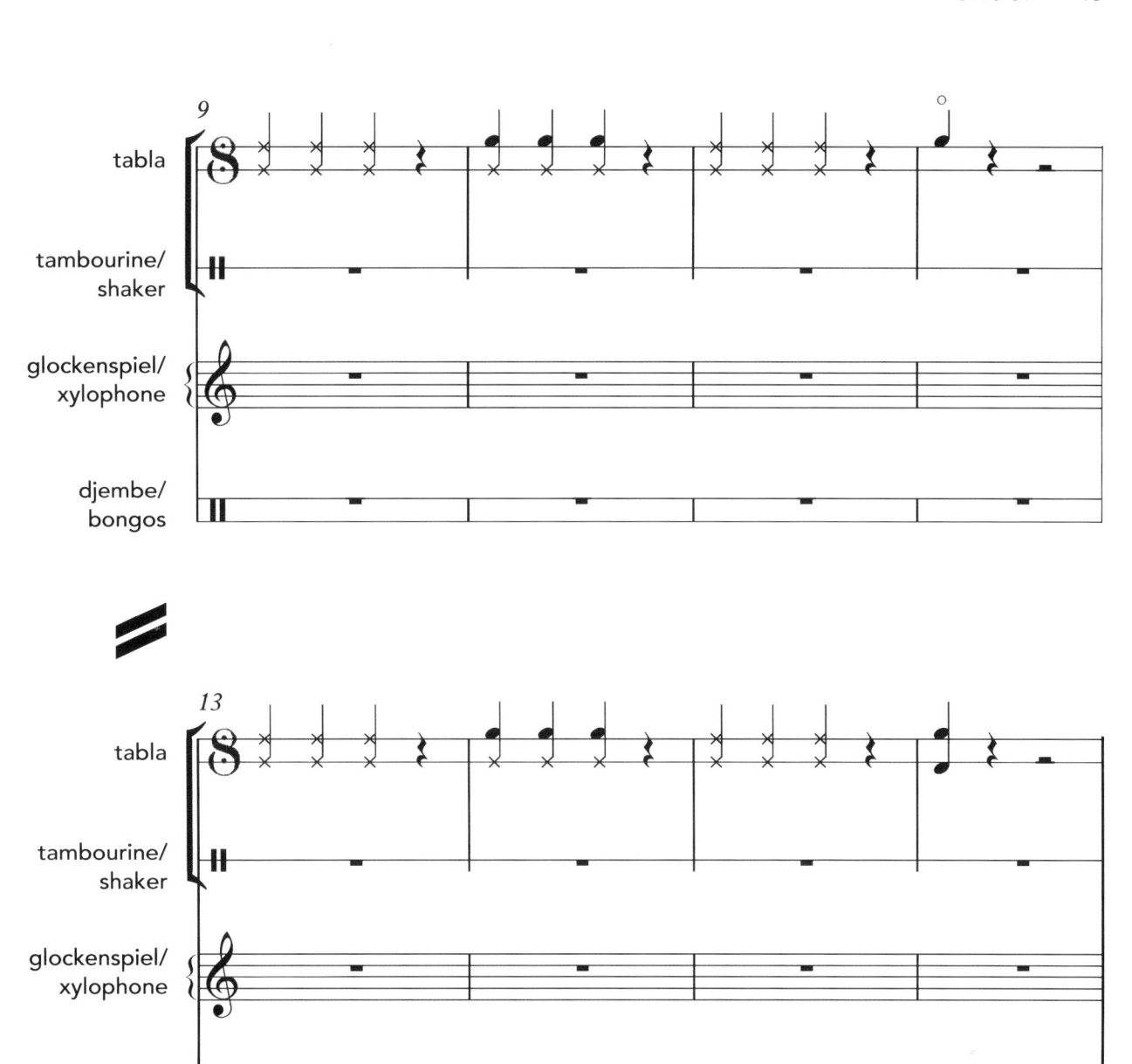

46 MODULE 2

GROUP 47

MODULE 2

GROUP 49

Group Piece 6

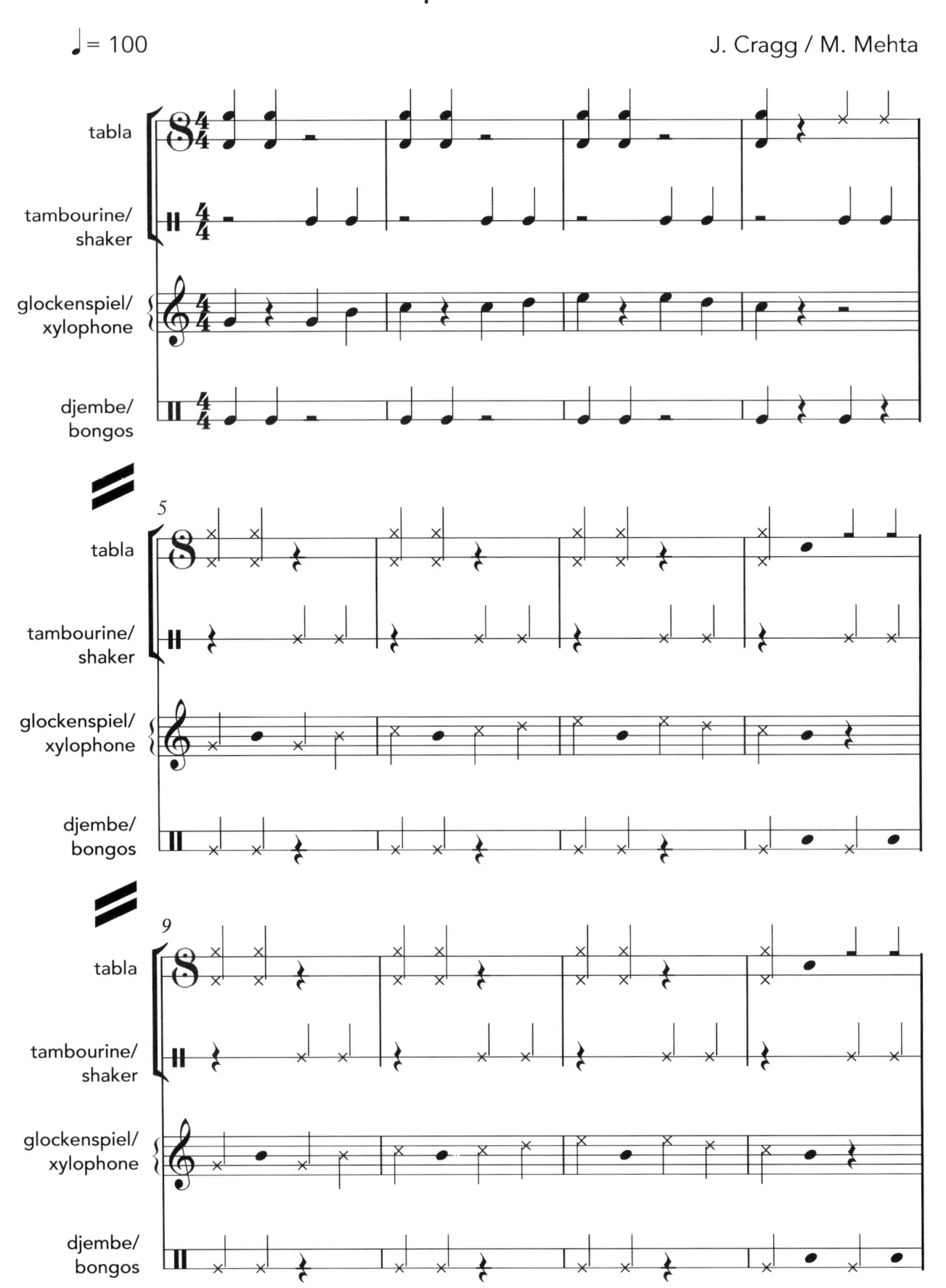

♩ = 100

J. Cragg / M. Mehta

13
tabla
tambourine/
shaker
glockenspiel/
xylophone
djembe/
bongos
17
tabla
tambourine/
shaker
glockenspiel/
xylophone
djembe/
bongos
21
tabla
tambourine/
shaker
glockenspiel/
xylophone
djembe/
bongos

25
tabla
tambourine/
shaker
glockenspiel/
xylophone
djembe/
bongos

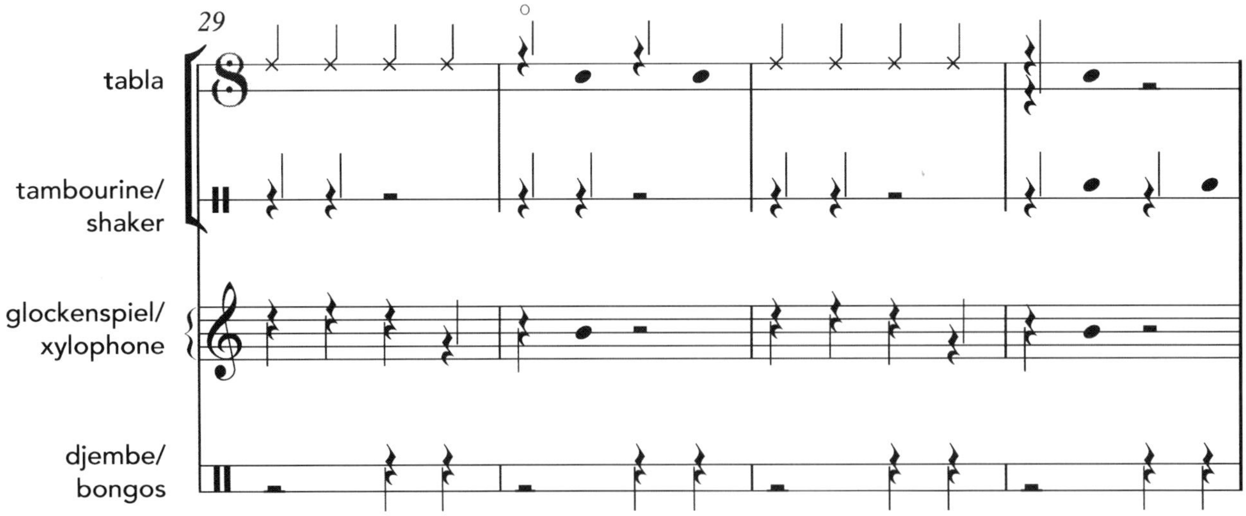
29
tabla
tambourine/
shaker
glockenspiel/
xylophone
djembe/
bongos

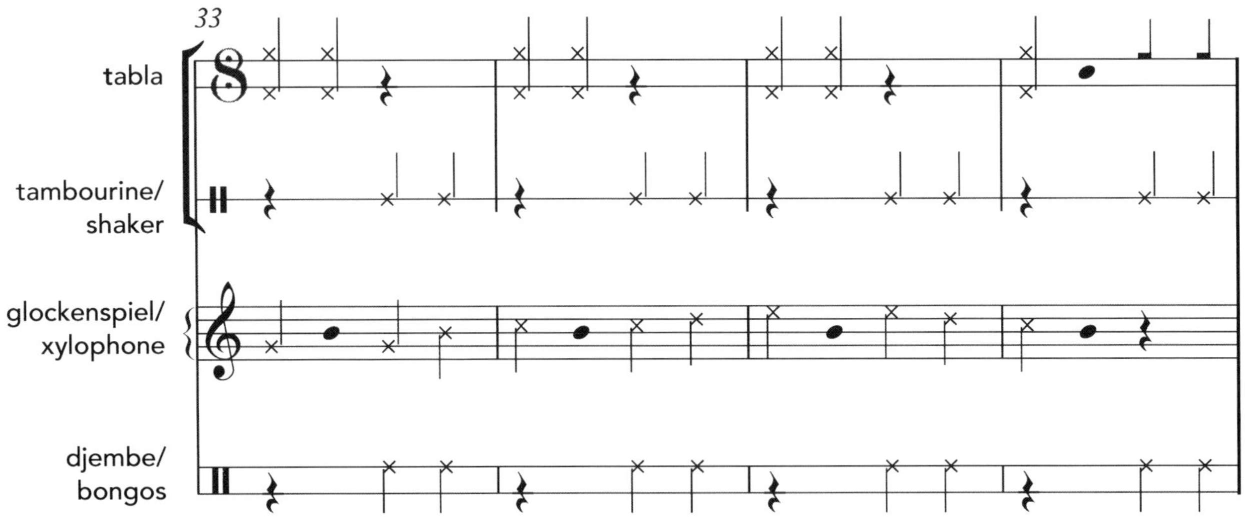
33
tabla
tambourine/
shaker
glockenspiel/
xylophone
djembe/
bongos

GROUP 53

Group Piece 7

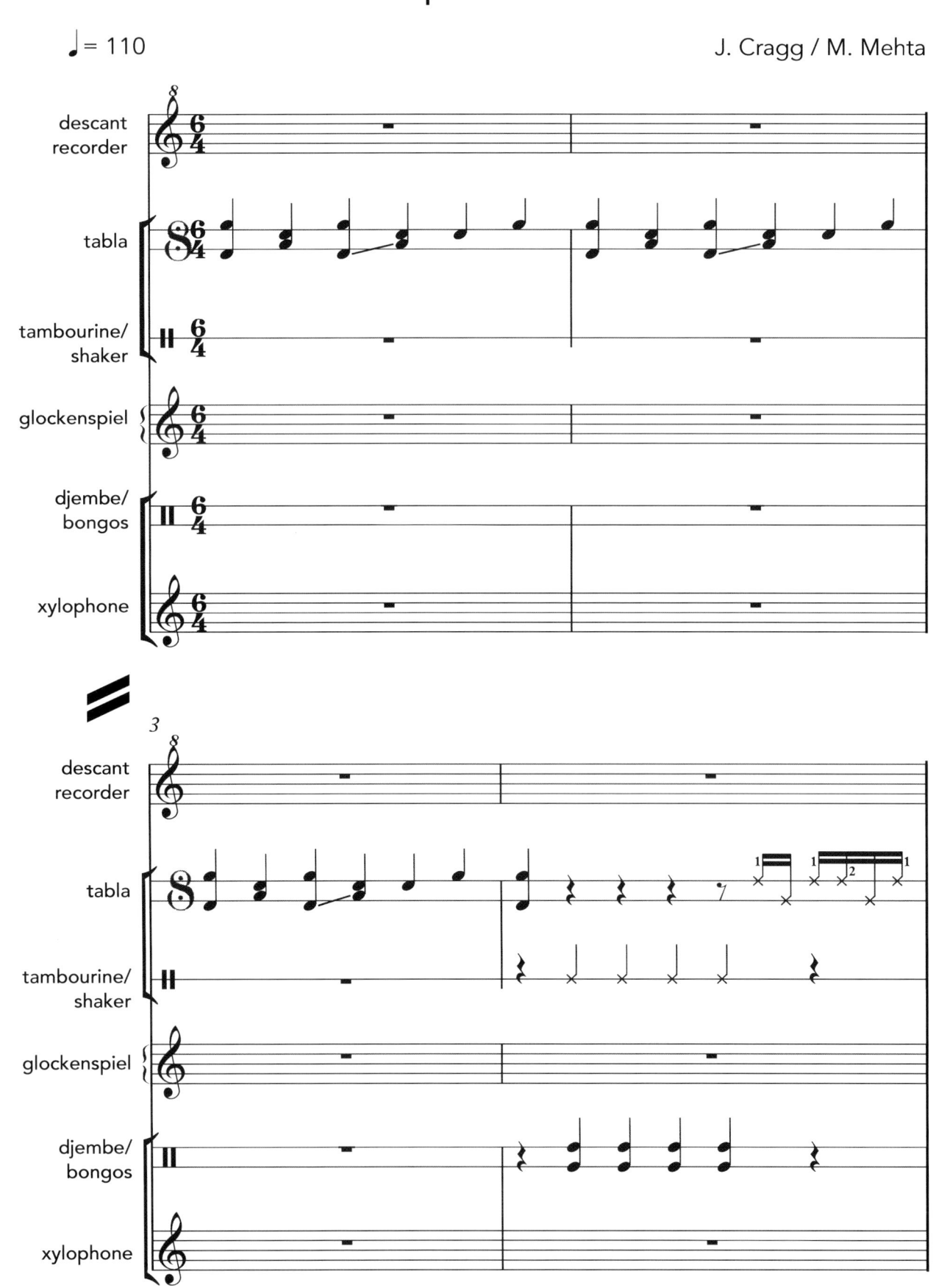

♩ = 110

J. Cragg / M. Mehta

copyright © Keda Music Ltd

GROUP 55

56 MODULE 2

GROUP 57

58 MODULE 2

GROUP 59

60 MODULE 2

29
descant recorder
tabla
tambourine/ shaker
glockenspiel
djembe/ bongos
xylophone

31
descant recorder
tabla
tambourine/ shaker
glockenspiel
djembe/ bongos
xylophone

62   MODULE 2

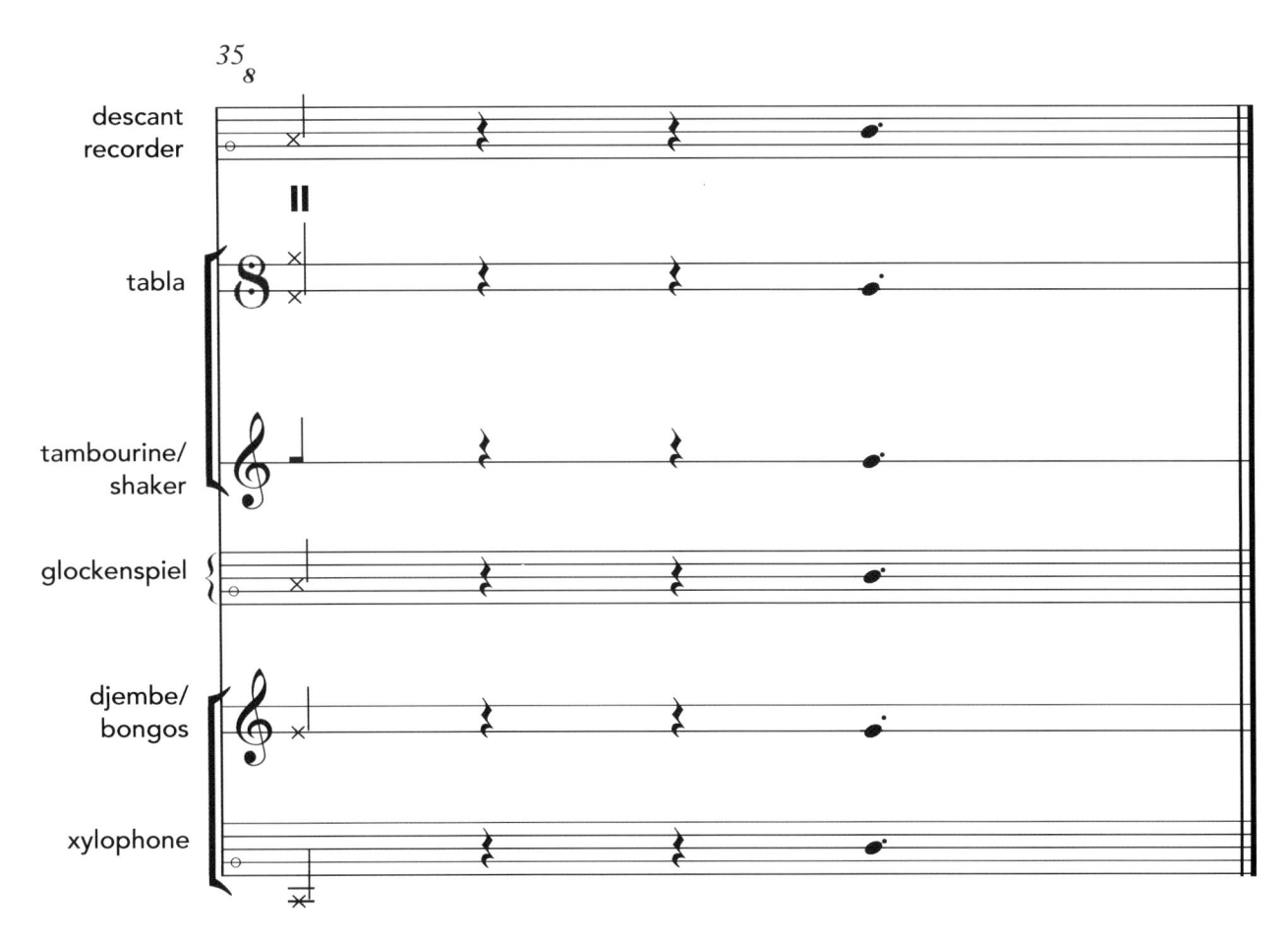

STRIKES & SOUNDS

Use the chart overleaf as a quick reference guide to all techniques and notations covered in this course. The online version also contains video demonstrations for each strike.

♩

Strikes & Sounds

LARGE DRUM

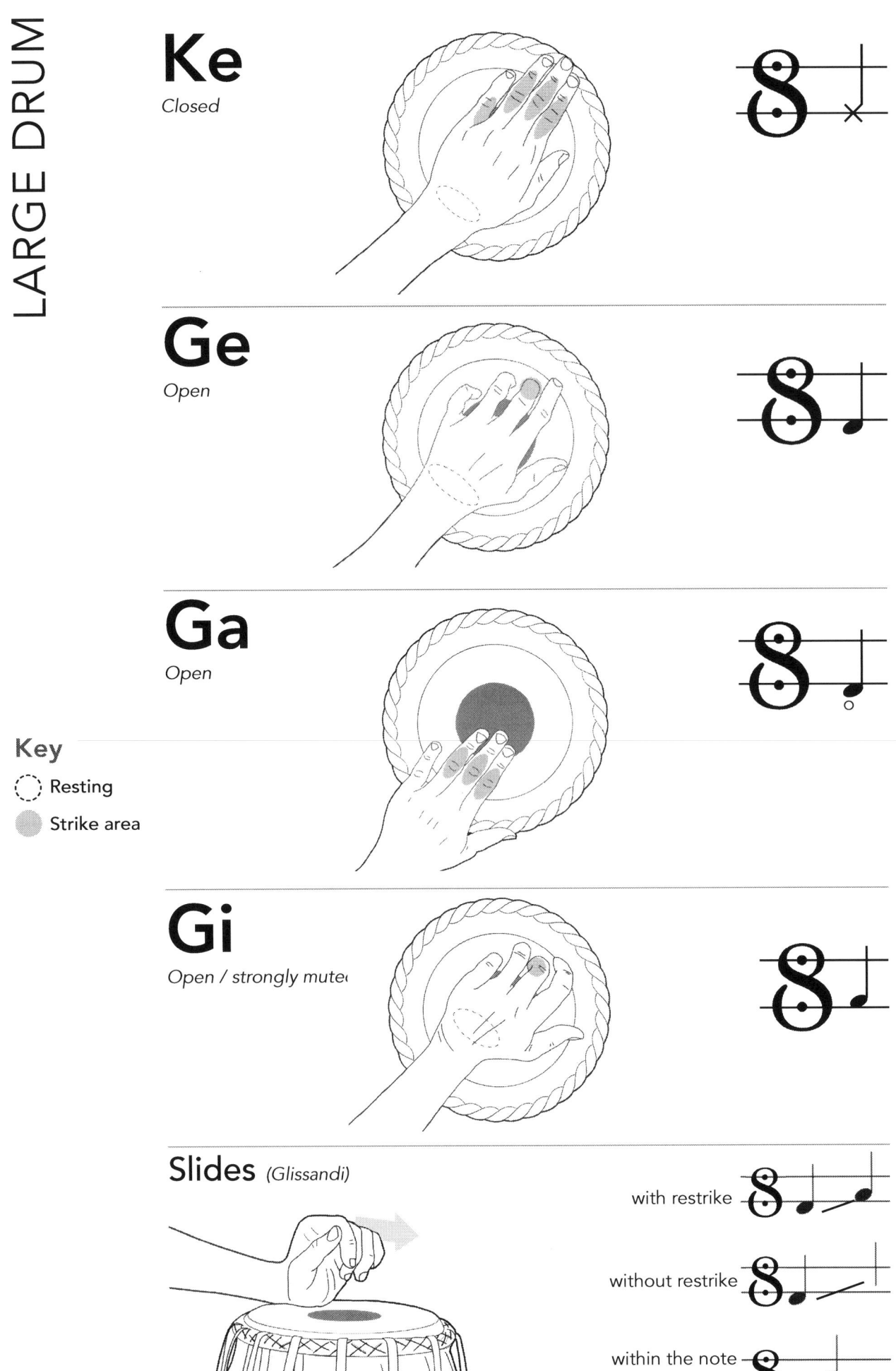

Ke
Closed

Ge
Open

Ga
Open

Key
- Resting
- Strike area

Gi
Open / strongly muted

Slides *(Glissandi)*

with restrike

without restrike

within the note

SECTION 65

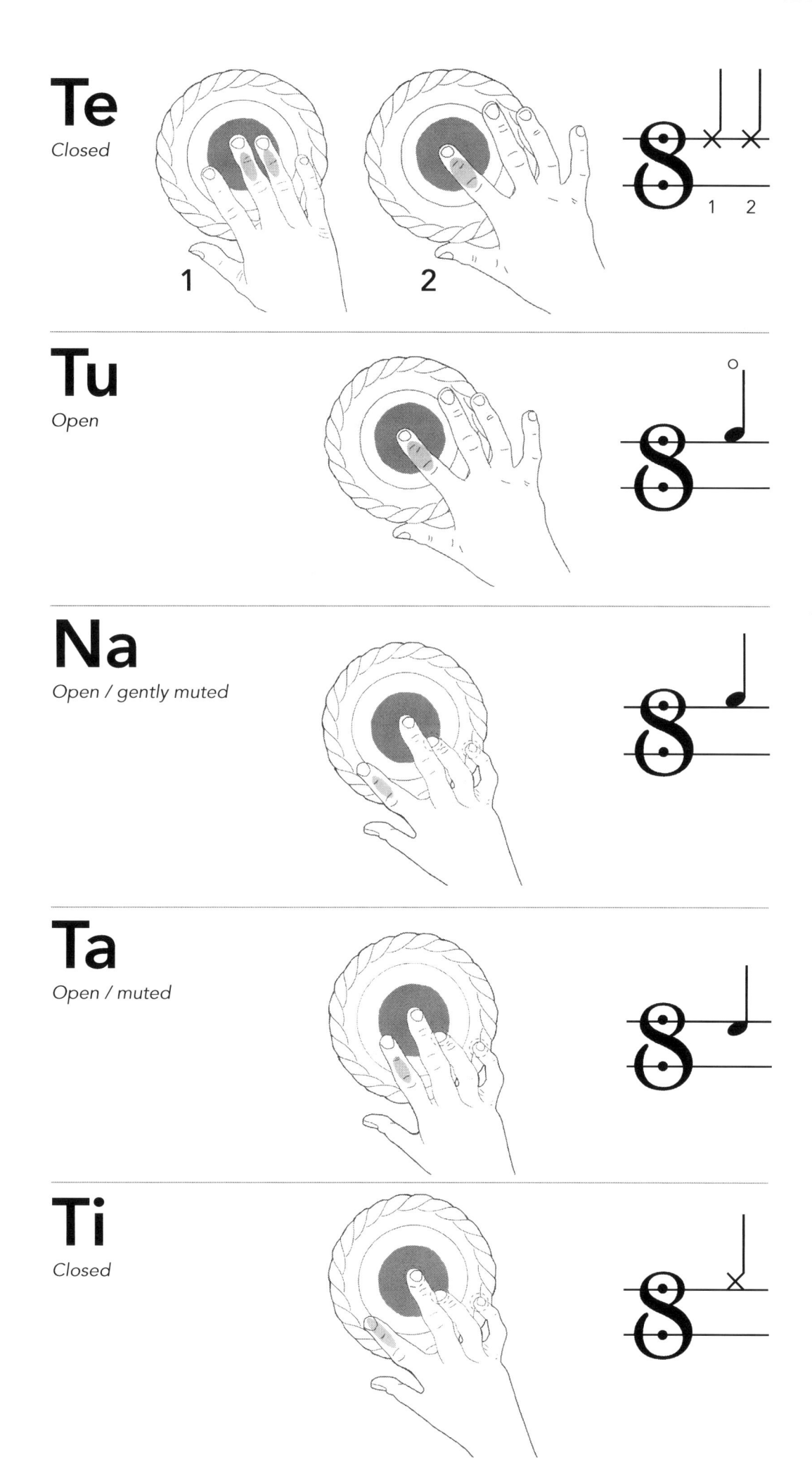

SMALLER DRUM

Te
Closed

1   2

Tu
Open

Na
Open / gently muted

Ta
Open / muted

Ti
Closed

READ & PLAY™

Well done for completing this part of this course. You are now ready to move to Module 3, where you will study rolls, tremolos and traditional rhythms.

keda.co.uk

Notes

Notes

Printed in Great Britain
by Amazon